Carousel Horses in Cross-Stitch

Carousel Horses in Cross-Stitch

Beautiful Projects for Every Month of the Year

Donna Kooler
with Linda Gillum
of Kooler Design Studio

A Sterling\Chapelle Book
Sterling Publishing Co., Inc. New York

Library of Congress Cataloging-in-Publication Data

Kooler, Donna.
    Carousel horses in cross-stitch : beautiful projects for every
month of the year. / Donna Kooler.
        p.   cm.
    Includes index.
    ISBN 0-8069-8836-3
    1. Cross-stitch--Patterns. 2. Merry-go-round art. I. Title.
TT778.C76K65   1992
746.44'3—dc20   92–38558
                                                            CIP

10 9 8 7 6 5 4 3 2 1

Published by Sterling Publishing Company, Inc.
387 Park Avenue South, New York, N.Y. 10016
Produced by Chapelle Ltd.
P.O. Box 9252, Newgate Station, Ogden, Utah 84409
© 1993 by Chapelle Ltd.
Distributed in Canada by Sterling Publishing
c/o Canadian Manda Group, P.O. Box 920, Station U
Toronto, Ontario, Canada M8Z 6P9
Distributed in Great Britain and Europe by Cassell PLC
Villiers House, 41/47 Strand, London WC2N 5JE, England
Distributed in Australia by Capricorn Link Ltd.
P.O. Box 665, Lane Cove, NSW 2066
Printed and Bound in Hong Kong
All rights reserved

Sterling ISBN 0-8069-8836-3

For Chapelle, Ltd.

Owners
Jo Packham and Terrece Beesley

Staff
Trice Boerens
Tina Annette Brady
Sandra Durbin Chapman
Holly Fuller
Kristi Glissmeyer
Susan Jorgensen
Margaret Shields Marti
Jackie McCowen
Barbara Milburn
Lisa Miles
Pamela Randall
Jennifer Roberts
Florence Stacey
Lorrie Young
Nancy Whitley
Gloria Zirkel

Photographer: *Ryne Hazen*

*Photographs in this book were
taken at
Anita Louise's Bear Lace
Cottage, Park City, Utah*

*Mary Gaskill's Trends &
Traditions, Ogden, Utah*

Jo Packham's home, Ogden, Utah

*Their cooperation and trust are
deeply appreciated.*

To Dr. Kaye,
Heartfelt thanks.
L. G.

About the designer

Through a friend, Linda Gillum discovered she could make a living doing something she loved — illustrating and designing for fine needlework. Nearly seven years ago, she teamed up with Donna Kooler, a former co-worker who had formed her own design business.

Linda loves the variety and challenge of her work with Kooler Design Studio, Inc., and also finds time for oil painting, watercolors and pastel drawings.

For the child in all of us , she has created the carousel samplers in this book. Linda is partial to natural subjects, such as animals and flowers. Her partiality is reflected in her fantastic yet realistic horses with their wealth of natural detail. Delightful, dramatic, whimsical and exquisite in this book, they carry us gaily through all the seasons and special times of our year.

There is nothing of greater value than real friends,
whose company brings simple pleasure.
Thank you, Doug, Linda and Joe, for being such friends.

About Kooler Design Studio, Inc.

With a rainbow of floss overflowing the shelves, Donna Kooler's California studio is as bright and appealing as a carousel. Instead of a carousel's tinny tinkle, however, there is soft background music, and rather than popcorn and cotton candy, an aromatic, homey kitchen.

One of Donna Kooler's greatest joys is providing an atmosphere that fosters creativity. Her co-workers, Linda Gillum, Barbara Baatz, Jorja Hernandez and Nancy Rossi, are surrounded by lovely cross-stitched designs and favorite books and mementos. They gaze through twelve-foot windows at the blue of the Pacific Ocean and the green of nearby Mount Diablo. As with any family, there is talk, laughter and lots of homemade cookies.

The studio is Donna Kooler's home-away-from-home. Its happy atmosphere, color and creativity help produce the invitingly rich designs we love to stitch.

Table Of Contents

An Enchanted January

An Enchanted January

An Enchanted January

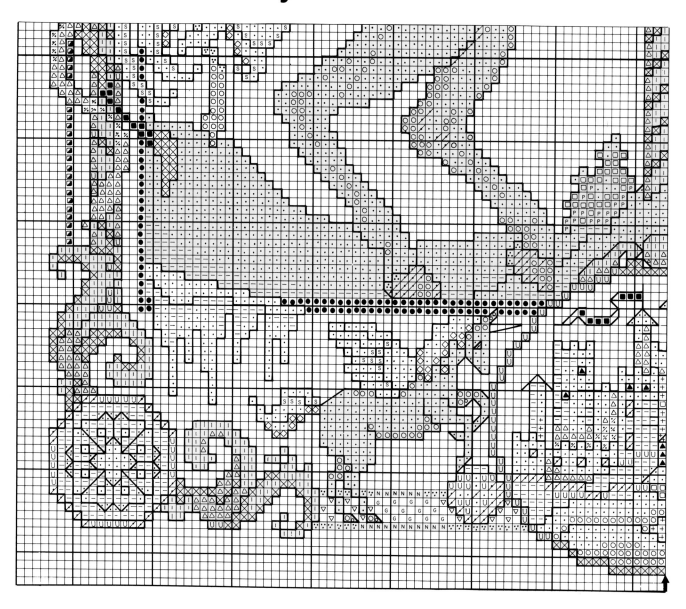

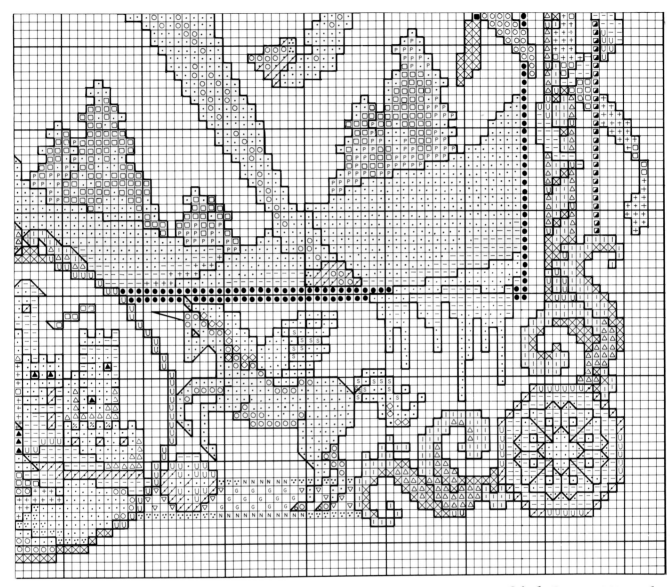

Stitch Count: 159 x 168

Model (see photo)
Stitched on forget-me-not blue Jobelan 28 over 2 threads, the finished design size is 11⅜" x 12". The fabric was cut 18" x 18".

FABRICS	DESIGN SIZES
Aida 11	14½" x 15¼"
Aida 14	11⅜" x 12"
Aida 18	8⅞" x 9⅜"
Hardanger 22	7¼" x 7⅝"

An Enchanted January

Model (see photo)
Stitched on forget-me-not blue Jobelan 28, over
2 threads, the finished design size is 11⅜" x 12".
The fabric was cut 18" x 18".

Anchor		DMC (used for sample)	
		Step 1: Cross-stitch (3 strands)	January
1			White
1		032	White (2 strands)+ Pearl Balger blending filament (1 strand)
300	K	745 / 091	Yellow-lt. pale (2 strands)+ Star Yellow Balger blending filament (1 strand)
301	▽	744 / 091	Yellow-pale (2 strands)+ Star Yellow Balger blending filament (1 strand)
891	E	676 / 091	Old Gold-lt. (2 strands)+ Star Yellow Balger blending filament (1 strand)
366	I	951	Peach Pecan-lt.
881	▵	945	Peach Beige
868		758	Terra Cotta-lt.
85 / 1	◇	3609 / White / 095	Plum-ultra lt. (2 strands)+ White (1 strand)+ Starburst Balger blending filament (1 strand)
85	G	3609	Plum-ultra lt.
85	✕	3609 / 093	Plum-ultra lt. (2 strands)+ Star Mauve Balger blending filament (1 strand)
86	▽	3608	Plum-vy. lt.
86	■	3608 / 093	Plum-vy. lt. (2 strands)+ Star Mauve Balger blending filament (1 strand)
108	◇	211	Lavender-lt.
108	+	211 / 093	Lavender-lt. (2 strands)+ Star Mauve Balger blending filament (1 strand)
108 / 1	S	211 / White / 095	Lavender-lt. (2 strands)+ White (1 strand)+ Starburst Balger blending filament (1 strand)
105	☐	209 / 012	Lavender-dk. (2 strands)+ Purple Balger blending filament (1 strand)
206	O	955 / 032	Nile Green-lt. (2 strands)+ Pearl Balger blending filament (1 strand)
203	☐	954	Nile Green
203	∴	954 / 032	Nile Green (2 strands)+ Pearl Balger blending filament (1 strand)
204	P	912	Emerald Green-lt.
186	∴	993	Aquamarine-lt.
186		993 / 032	Aquamarine-lt. (2 strands)+ Pearl Balger blending filament (1 strand)
185	N	964	Seagreen-lt.
185	▵	964 / 032	Seagreen-lt. (2 strands)+ Pearl Balger blending filament (1 strand)
187	◼	958	Seagreen-dk.
158	–	775	Baby Blue-vy. lt.
158	–	775 / 014	Baby Blue-vy. lt. (2 strands)+ Sky Blue Balger blending filament (1 strand)
159	+	3325	Baby Blue-lt.
159	U	3325 / 094	Baby Blue-lt. (2 strands)+ Star Blue Balger blending filament (1 strand)
145		334 / 006	Baby Blue-med. (2 strands)+ Blue Balger blending filament (1 strand)
131	●	798	Delft-dk.
131	▲	798 / 006	Delft-dk. (2 strands)+ Blue Balger blending filament (1 strand)
347	✕	402	Mahogany-vy. lt.
324	U	922	Copper-lt.
351	W	400	Mahogany-dk.
381	◆	838	Beige Brown-vy. dk.
397	O	762	Pearl Gray-vy. lt.
397	✓	762 / 032	Pearl Gray-vy. lt. (2 strands)+ Pearl Balger blending filament (1 strand)
399	╱	318	Steel Gray-lt.
399	∴	318 / 032	Steel Gray-lt. (2 strands)+ Pearl Balger blending filament (1 strand)
400	∴	317	Pewter Gray

		Step 2: Backstitch (1 strand)	
		002P	Gold Balger cable (2 strands) (lightning bolt)
145		334	Baby Blue-med. (saddle, clouds, raindrops, owl masks, teal, green, blue and white streamers, bridle, crupper, wing, snowflakes in air, trees, snow, icicles, castle, large and small medallions, breast collar, crystal ball)
145		334	Baby Blue-med. (2 strands) (snowflakes on horse, wind)
349		301	Mahogany-med. (moon, scroll-work, poles, hand, circle around castle, wrinkles and mouth of Old Man Winter, owl eyes and beaks, yellow on unicorn)
381		838	Beige Brown-vy. dk. (Old Man Winter s face, unicorn eye)
400		317	Pewter Gray (all else)

Wise Up!

Model (see photo)
Stitched on forget-me-not blue Jobelan 28 over 2 threads, the finished design size is 2⅞" x 2⅜". The fabric was cut 9" x 9".

FABRICS	DESIGN SIZES
Aida 11	3⅝" x 3"
Aida 14	2⅞" x 2⅜"
Aida 18	2¼" x 1⅞"
Hardanger 22	1⅞" x 1½"

Materials
Completed design on forget-me-not blue Jobelan 28
Two 6" squares of blue pinstripe fabric; matching thread
Two 25" x 2" x ¾" weathered wood pieces
Two 21" x 2" x ¾" weathered wood pieces
1⅝" wooden bunny cutout (without ears)
1⅛" wooden bunny cutout (without ears)
Purchased frame with a 3⅝" x 3" window
3"–5" twig
Blue acrylic paint
¼ yard of ⅛"-wide pink satin ribbon
Small amount of polyester stuffing
19" x 15" Masonite piece
Small-print wallpaper scraps
2" x 3½" x ¼" wood piece
Four 2½" x 3½" x ¼" wood pieces
12¾" moulding piece
5"-diameter small basket, sawed in half (see photo)
Assorted small, dried flowers
Tracing paper
Dressmaker's pen
Wood glue
Hot-glue gun and glue

Directions
Seams are ¼".

1. Paint weathered wood pieces, bunny cutouts, and ready-made frame with a thin wash of blue paint. Allow to dry. Cut design piece to measure 4½" x 3¾". Place in ready-made frame, following manufacturer's instructions. Hot-glue twig in place as desired so owl appears perched on branches. Set aside.

2. Make patterns. Cut two of each pattern from one pinstripe square. Stitch each matching ear with right sides facing, leaving an opening for turning. Clip curves and turn. Stuff sparingly; slipstitch opening closed. Hot-glue small ear to small bunny cutout and large ear to large cutout. Cut ribbon in half and tie each half into a bow, hot-gluing one bow to neck of each bunny. Set aside.

3. With remaining pinstripe square, machine-stitch ½" from each raw edge for basket liner. Pull threads outside stitching to make fringe. Arrange liner and dried flowers in basket half (see photo); glue. Set aside.

4. Glue wallpaper to smooth side of Masonite. Consult a professional framer for assistance in framing Masonite with painted wood pieces, making sure outside edges of each are aligned.

5. Glue short wood pieces and moulding to Masonite to resemble a kitchen counter with wood glue. Hot-glue miniature framed piece, bunnies and filled basket half to Masonite. See photo for placement.

Large ear pattern

Small ear pattern

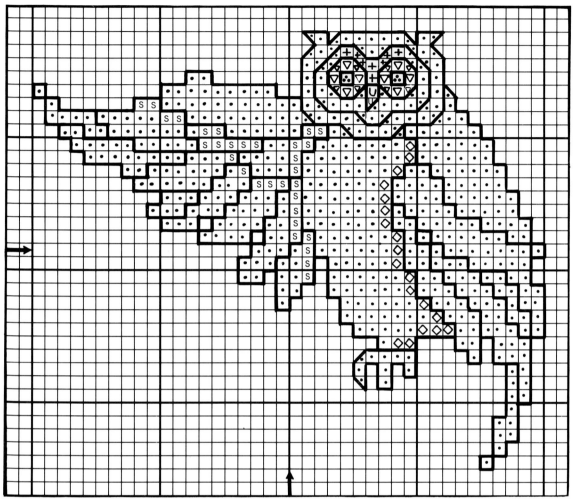

Stitch Count: 40 x 33

Anchor   **DMC (used for sample)**

Step 1: Cross-stitch (3 strands)

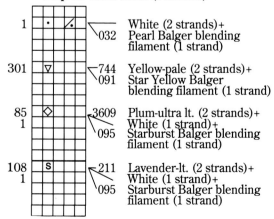

1	· /	032	White (2 strands)+ Pearl Balger blending filament (1 strand)
301	▽	744 091	Yellow-pale (2 strands)+ Star Yellow Balger blending filament (1 strand)
85 1	◇	3609 095	Plum-ultra lt. (2 strands)+ White (1 strand)+ Starburst Balger blending filament (1 strand)
108 1	S	211 095	Lavender-lt. (2 strands)+ White (1 strand)+ Starburst Balger blending filament (1 strand)

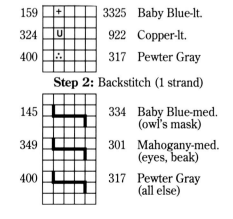

159	+	3325	Baby Blue-lt.
324	U	922	Copper-lt.
400	∴	317	Pewter Gray

Step 2: Backstitch (1 strand)

145		334	Baby Blue-med. (owl's mask)
349		301	Mahogany-med. (eyes, beak)
400		317	Pewter Gray (all else)

17

February Forever

ROYAL CIRCUS

February Forever

February Forever

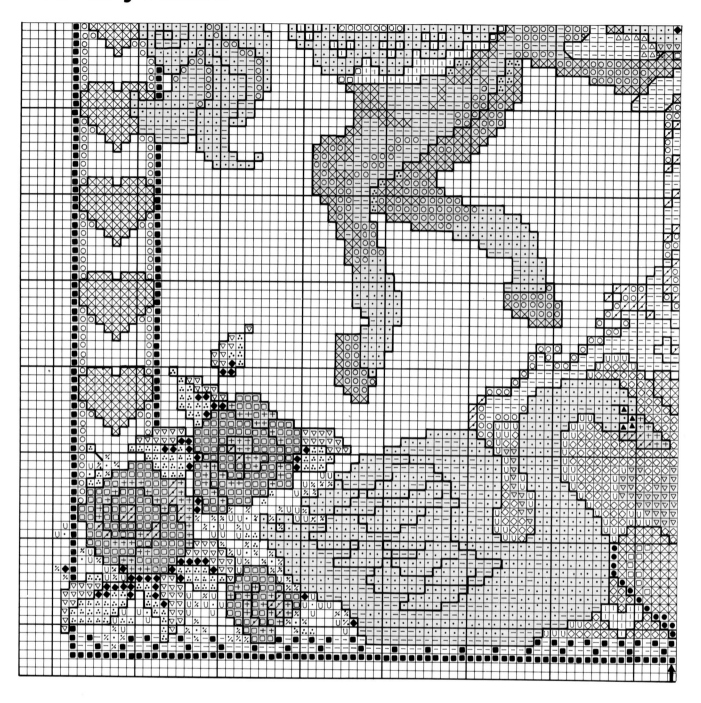

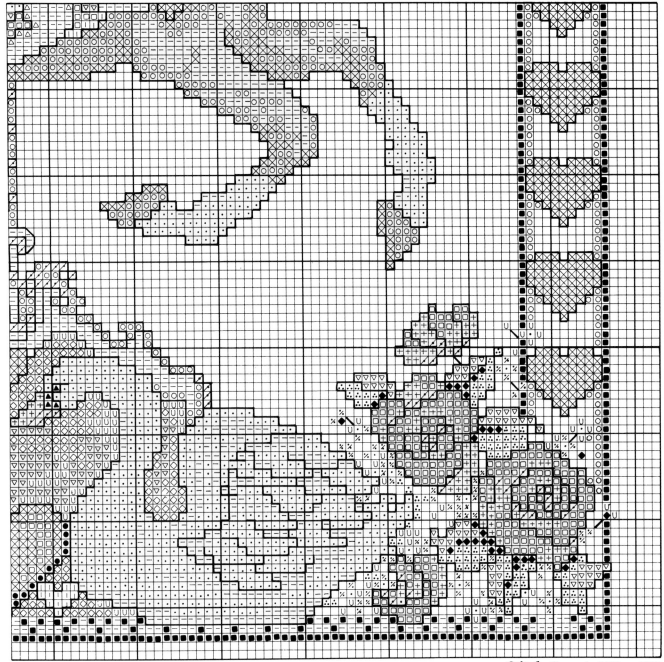

Stitch Count: 153 x 170

February Forever

Model (see photo)
Stitched on sandstone Linen 28 over
2 threads, the finished design size is
10⅞" x 12⅛". The fabric was cut 17" x 19".

FABRICS	DESIGN SIZES
Aida 11	13⅞" x 15½"
Aida 14	10⅞" x 12⅛"
Aida 18	8½" x 9½"
Hardanger 22	7" x 7¾"

Anchor   **DMC (used for sample)**

Step 1: Cross-stitch (3 strands)

Anchor			DMC	Color
1	·	╱		White
301	·		744	Yellow-pale
886	+	╱	3047	Yellow Beige-lt.
891	N	◥	677	Old Gold-vy. lt.
881	–	╱	945	Peach Beige
868	△	◢	758	Terra Cotta-lt.
8	▢	◿	353	Peach
10	+	╱	352	Coral-lt.
11	╱	╱	350	Coral-med.
24	I	╱	776	Pink-med.
27	▢		899	Rose-med.
46	✕		666	Christmas Red-bright
20	●		498	Christmas Red-dk.
108	G		211	Lavender-lt.
105	R		209	Lavender-dk.
158	▽	◿	775	Baby Blue-vy. lt.
159	◇		827	Blue-vy. lt.
130	U		799	Delft-med.
131	╱		798	Delft-dk.
265	▽		3348	Yellow Green-lt.

Anchor			DMC	Color
266	∴		3347	Yellow Green-med.
268	◆		3345	Hunter Green-dk.
347	○	◿	402	Mahogany-vy. lt.
324	╱	╱	922	Copper-lt.
339	■	◢	920	Copper-med.
351	◩		400	Mahogany-dk.
397	–	╱	762	Pearl Gray-vy. lt.
399	○	◿	318	Steel Gray-lt.
400	✕	◢	317	Pewter Gray
401	∴	◿	413	Pewter Gray-dk.
403	▲	◿	310	Black

Step 2: Backstitch (1 strand)

Anchor		DMC	Color
11		350	Coral-med. (salmon ribbons and flowers, swan beaks)
46		666	Christmas Red-bright (2 strands) (lettering)
20		498	Christmas Red-dk. (hearts, red bow, saddle, bridle, pink design in white on crupper)
105		209	Lavender-dk. (lavender flowers in cupid's hand)
130		799	Delft-med. (cupids' clothing, white flowers at top, doves)
268		3345	Hunter Green-dk. (stems, leaves)
351		400	Mahogany-dk. (cupids, carousel pole)
400		317	Pewter Gray (horse, cupids' wings, swans)
403		310	Black (horse eye)

Step 3: French Knot (1 strand)

Anchor		DMC	Color
46	■	666	Christmas Red-bright
130	●	799	Delft-med.

Cupids' Treasure Box

Model (see photo)
Stitched on cream Hardanger 22 over 2 threads, the finished design size is 5¾" x 4⅝". The fabric was cut 14" x 12".

FABRICS	DESIGN SIZES
Aida 11	5¾" x 4⅝"
Aida 14	4½" x 3⅝"
Aida 18	3½" x 2⅞"
Hardanger 22	2⅞" x 2⅜"

Anchor		DMC (used for sample)	
Step 1: Cross-stitch (3 strands)			
1			White
881		945	Peach Beige
868		758	Terra Cotta-lt.
24		776	Pink-med.
46		666	Christmas Red-bright
108		211	Lavender-lt.
105		209	Lavender-dk.
158		775	Baby Blue-vy. lt.
130		799	Delft-med.
266		3347	Yellow Green-med.
347		402	Mahogany-vy. lt.
324		922	Copper-lt.
339		920	Copper-med.
397		762	Pearl Gray-vy. lt.
Step 2: Backstitch (1 strand)			
130		799	Delft-med. (clothing)
351		400	Mahogany-dk. (flowers, heart, cupids' bodies)
400		317	Pewter Gray (wings)

Materials
Completed design piece on cream Hardanger 22; matching thread
½ yard of print fabric; matching thread
½ yard of fleece
Mat board
1¼ yards of ¼"-wide gray ribbon
¼ yard of ⅛"-wide blue ribbon; matching thread
⅛ yard of ⅛"-wide black ribbon; matching thread
Four small red heart buttons
Glue

Directions
Seams are ¼".

1. Cut the following from mat board: two 7¾" x 5¾" pieces, one each for lid and bottom; two 7 ¾" x 3¼" sides; and two 5¾" x 3¼" ends.

2. Cut design piece 8½" x 6½" with design centered. From gray ribbon, cut two 8½" lengths, two 6½" lengths and five 3" lengths. Pin 6½" lengths with ribbon edge ½" from design piece edges. Repeat with longer pieces. Place one 3" piece diagonally across opposite corners; see photo. Cut two lengths of black ribbon; pin parallel to gray ribbon toward corners. Cut two 4½" lengths of blue ribbon; pin parallel to gray ribbon toward design. Slipstitch all ribbon to design piece.

3. From print fabric, cut the following: three 8½" x 6½" pieces, one for lid and two for bottom; two 7½" x 8½" sides; and two 7½" x 6½" ends. Cut one fleece piece to match the design piece and each print piece listed above.

4. Match fleece pieces to corresponding design piece or print piece. To make lid, place design/fleece piece and one print/fleece piece with right sides facing. Stitch on three sides. Trim fleece

26

from seam allowances. Turn. Insert mat board lid. Fold seam allowance of opening to inside and slipstitch opening closed. Set lid aside. Repeat for bottom.

5. Fold one end/fleece piece in half to measure 3¾" wide. Stitch both 3¾" edges. Trim fleece from seam allowances. Turn. Insert mat board end. Fold seam allowance to inside and slipstitch opening closed. Repeat with remaining end and two side pieces.

6. Whipsitch ends and sides together on short edges, making frame for box. Whipstitch bottom to frame. Place lid on box and whipstitch back edge only.

7. To make clasp, thread a button onto each end of one remaining gray ribbon length; glue ribbon ends to button backs. Fold ribbon into loop. Tack loop to center box front (Diagram). Thread two buttons onto another remaining ribbon length. Glue ribbon ends together and tack in center to form two loops, centering one button on each loop. Tack to center front lid edge. Tie remaining ribbon into small bow and glue to lid over looped ribbon. Trim ends.

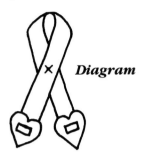

Diagram

Stitch Count: 63 x 51

March-Go-Round

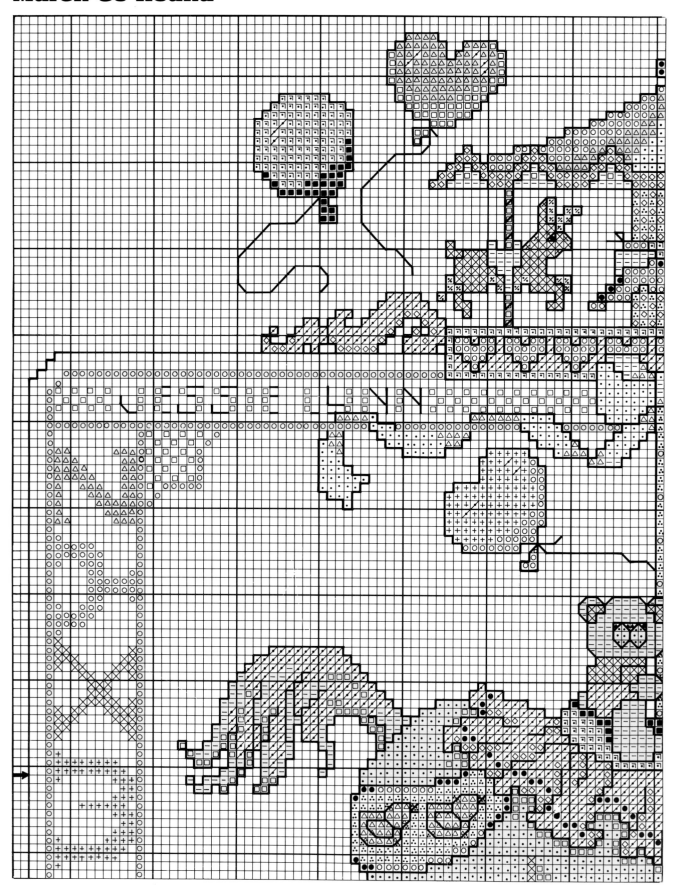

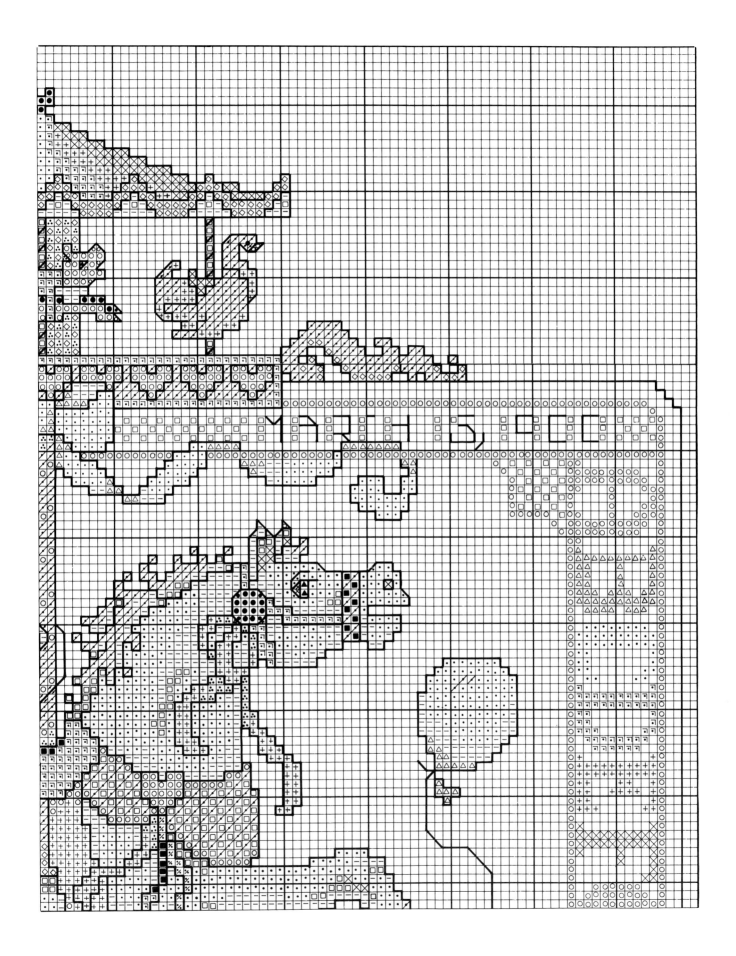

March-Go-Round

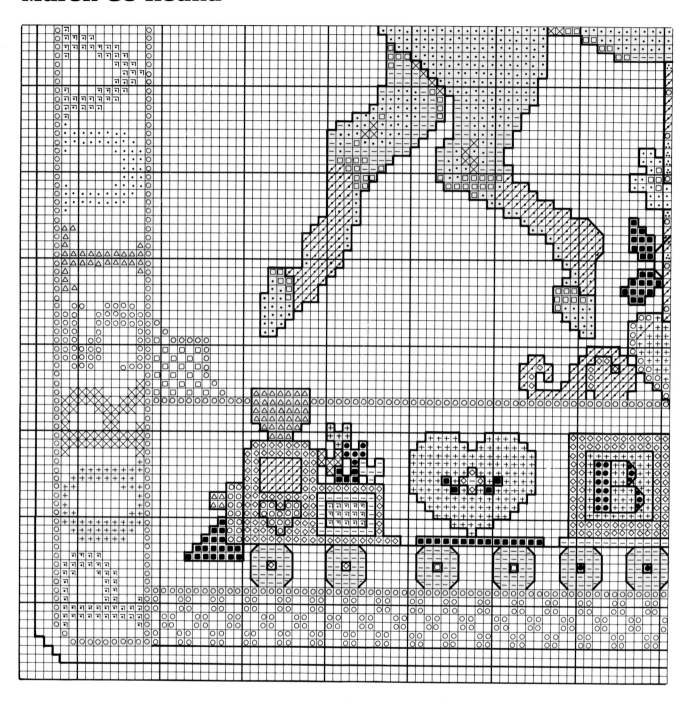

Stitch Count: 153 x 172

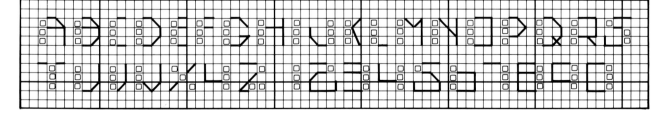

March-Go-Round

Model (see photo)
Stitched on white Aida 14, the finished
design size is 10⅞" x 12¼". The fabric was
cut 17" x 19".

FABRICS	DESIGN SIZES
Aida 11	13⅞" x 15⅝"
Aida 18	8½" x 9½"
Hardanger 22	7" x 7⅞"

Anchor   **DMC (used for sample)**

Step 1: Cross-stitch (2 strands)

Anchor			DMC	
1	/	/		White
300	·	/	745	Yellow-lt. pale
301	–		744	Yellow-pale
297	△		743	Yellow-med.
8	△		353	Peach
10	□	/	352	Coral-lt.
48	+	/	818	Baby Pink
24	O	/	776	Pink-med.
27	●	/	899	Rose-med.
85	X	/	3609	Plum-ultra lt.
86	⁒		3608	Plum-vy. lt.
158	∴	/	775	Baby Blue-vy. lt.
159	◇		3325	Baby Blue-lt.
145	O		334	Baby Blue-med.
160	+	/	3761	Sky Blue-lt.
167	∴	/	3766	Peacock Blue-lt.
206	◗	/	955	Nile Green-lt.
203	■		954	Nile Green
885	·		739	Tan-ultra vy. lt.
942	–	/	738	Tan-vy. lt.
362	□		437	Tan-lt.
363	X	/	436	Tan
905	▲	/	3031	Mocha Brown-vy. dk.

Step 2: Backstitch (1 strand)

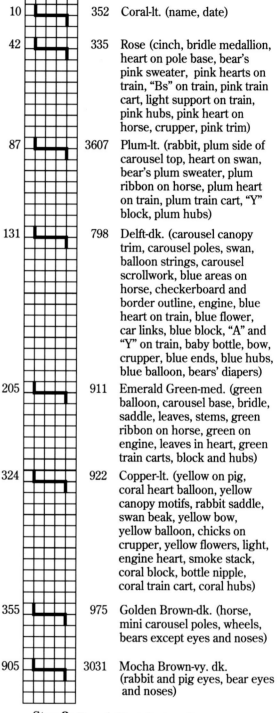

Anchor	DMC	
10	352	Coral-lt. (name, date)
42	335	Rose (cinch, bridle medallion, heart on pole base, bear's pink sweater, pink hearts on train, "Bs" on train, pink train cart, light support on train, pink hubs, pink heart on horse, crupper, pink trim)
87	3607	Plum-lt. (rabbit, plum side of carousel top, heart on swan, bear's plum sweater, plum ribbon on horse, plum heart on train, plum train cart, "Y" block, plum hubs)
131	798	Delft-dk. (carousel canopy trim, carousel poles, swan, balloon strings, carousel scrollwork, blue areas on horse, checkerboard and border outline, engine, blue heart on train, blue flower, car links, blue block, "A" and "Y" on train, baby bottle, bow, crupper, blue ends, blue hubs, blue balloon, bears' diapers)
205	911	Emerald Green-med. (green balloon, carousel base, bridle, saddle, leaves, stems, green ribbon on horse, green on engine, leaves in heart, green train carts, block and hubs)
324	922	Copper-lt. (yellow on pig, coral heart balloon, yellow canopy motifs, rabbit saddle, swan beak, yellow bow, yellow balloon, chicks on crupper, yellow flowers, light, engine heart, smoke stack, coral block, bottle nipple, coral train cart, coral hubs)
355	975	Golden Brown-dk. (horse, mini carousel poles, wheels, bears except eyes and noses)
905	3031	Mocha Brown-vy. dk. (rabbit and pig eyes, bear eyes and noses)

Step 3: French Knot (1 strand)

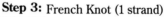
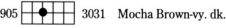

Anchor	DMC	
905	●	3031	Mocha Brown-vy. dk.

Greetings, Baby!

Model (see photo)

Stitched on white Perforated Paper 14, the finished design size is 4⅛" x 2⅝". The paper was cut 15" x 12". Center design horizontally and begin stitching 1" below 15" edge of paper.

FABRICS	DESIGN SIZES
Aida 11	5¼" x 3⅜"
Aida 14	4⅛" x 2⅝"
Aida 18	3¼" x 2"
Hardanger 22	2⅝" x 1⅝"

Materials

Completed design on white Perforated Paper 14
Two 18" x 12" pieces of unstitched white Perforated Paper 14
One 20" x 14" x ¼" Masonite piece
2 yards of ½"-wide pink multi-colored twisted cotton cording
⅝ yard of cream lace trim
Wood cut-outs for decorating
Spray adhesive
Tracing paper
Dressmaker's pen
Wood glue
Hot-glue gun and glue

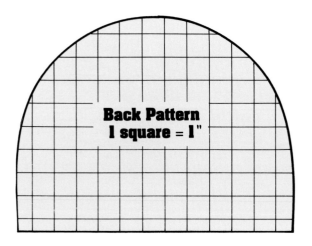

Back Pattern
1 square = 1"

Directions

1. Make pattern. From perforated paper, cut design piece for back slightly larger than pattern, two 3½" x 3"sides and one 12½" x 3" front. From Masonite, cut one back according to pattern, two 3" squares for sides, one 12" x 3" bottom and one 12½"x 3" front.

2. Glue design piece to smooth side of Masonite back with spray adhesive, centering top of design ⅜" from top edge. Trim perforated paper with knife, working from back side. Set aside.

3. With smooth sides out, glue a Masonite side to each end of bottom with wood glue. Then glue front to bottom/sides to make holder (Diagram).

4. With spray adhesive, glue paper front to holder front and each paper side to holder sides, matching edges. Trim perforated paper with knife, working from back side.

5. Glue holder to papered back with wood glue and all edges aligned.

6. Leaving a 3" tail, begin hot gluing cording to top right edge of holder at back, continuing around top curved edge of back and ending where gluing began. Cut cording, leaving a 4" tail. Knot all ends. Make a bow with remaining cording. Glue bow where gluing began (see photo). Hot glue lace flush with top edge of holder sides and front, gluing cut-outs as desired.

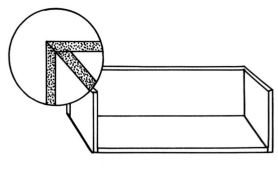

Diagram

Anchor   DMC (used for sample)

Step 1: Cross-stitch (2 strands)

1				White
300			745	Yellow-lt. pale
301			744	Yellow-pale
8			353	Peach
10			352	Coral-lt.
24			776	Pink-med.
27			899	Rose-med.
85			3609	Plum-ultra lt.
86			3608	Plum-vy. lt.
160			3761	Sky Blue-lt.
158			775	Baby Blue-vy. lt.
159			3325	Baby Blue-lt.
206			955	Nile Green-lt.
362			437	Tan-lt.
905			3031	Mocha Brown-vy. dk.

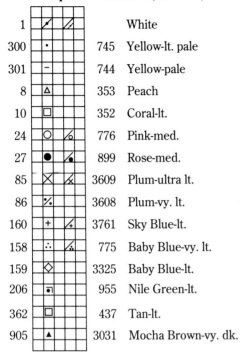

Step 2: Backstitch (1 strand)

10		352	Coral-lt. (yellow edges on carousel, saddle on rabbit, crupper, bridle on pig, swan beak)
42		335	Rose (pink edge of carousel, pig, hearts)
87		3607	Plum-lt. (plum edge on carousel, rabbit, swan saddle)
131		798	Delft-dk. (carousel canopy trim, blue pole, swan)
205		911	Emerald Green-med. (saddle on pig, carousel base)
355		975	Golden Brown-dk. (mini carousel poles)
905		3031	Mocha Brown-vy. dk. (rabbit and pig eyes)

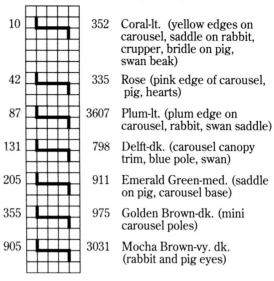

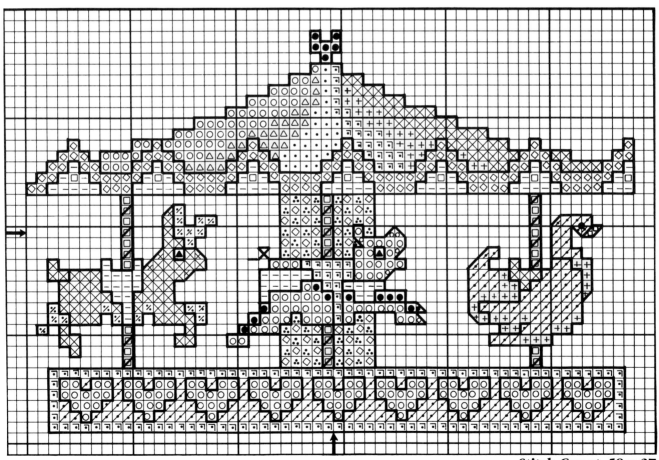

Stitch Count: 58 x 37

"Egg"stra Special April

"Egg"stra Special April

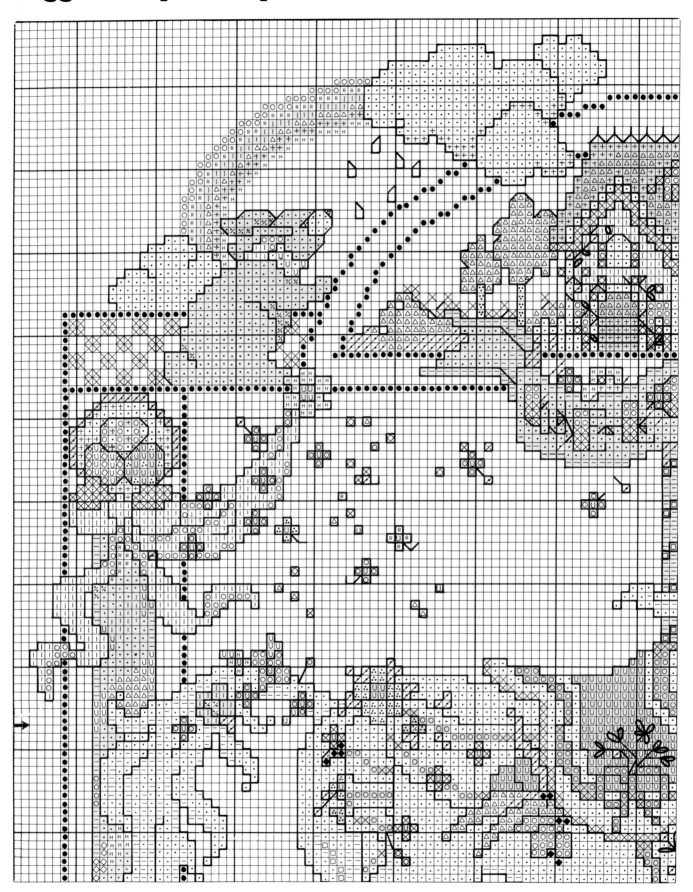

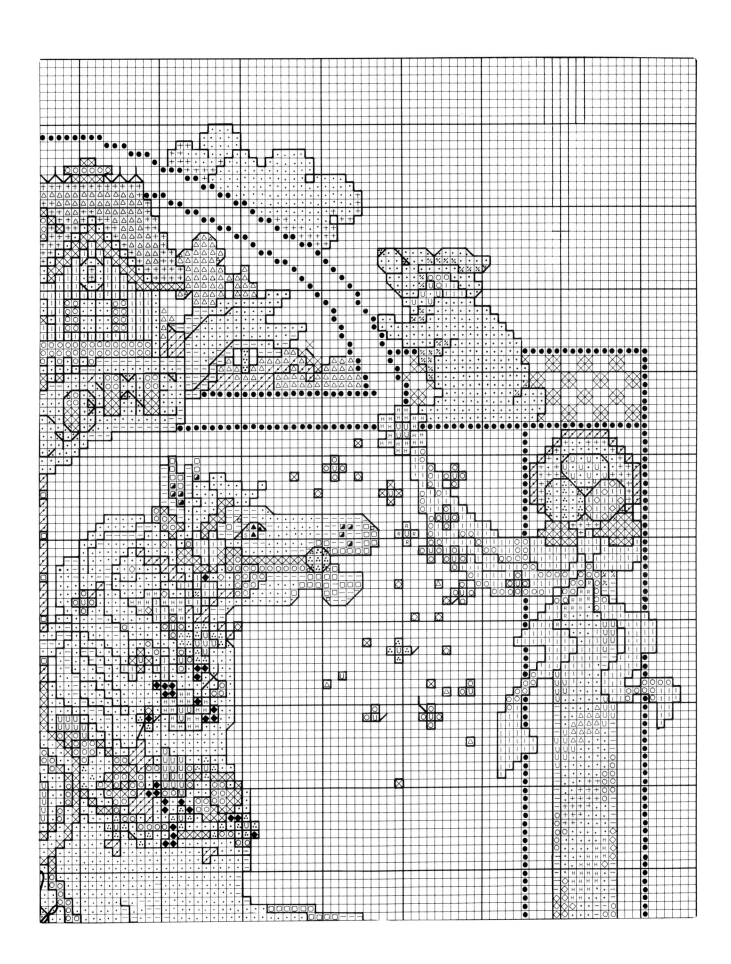

"Egg"stra Special April

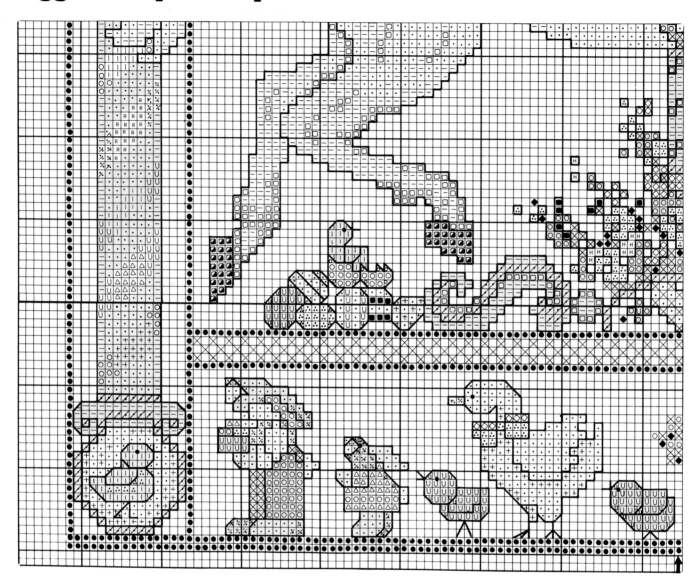

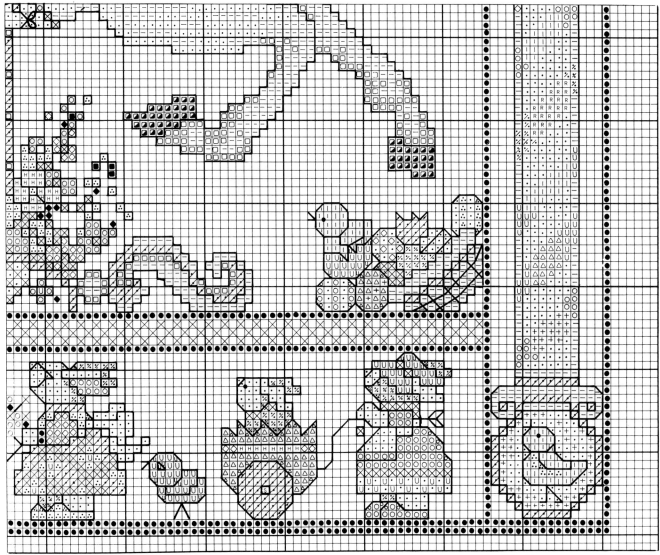

Stitch Count: 161 x 166

"Egg"stra Special April

Model (see photo)
Stitched on honeysuckle pink Aida 14, the finished design size is 11½" x 11⅞". The fabric was cut 18" x 18".

FABRICS	DESIGN SIZES
Aida 11	14⅝" x 15⅛"
Aida 18	9" x 9¼"
Hardanger 22	7⅜" x 7½"

Anchor   **DMC** (used for sample)

Step 1: Cross-stitch (3 strands)

Anchor			DMC	Color
1	·	∕		White
300	I	∕	745	Yellow-lt. pale
301	U	∕	744	Yellow-pale
297	∴	∕	743	Yellow-med.
8	R		353	Peach
10	⁒		352	Coral-lt.
48	I	∕	818	Baby Pink
24	O	∕	776	Pink-med.
76	X	∕	962	Wild Rose-med.
86	∴	∕	3608	Plum-vy. lt.
108	H	∕	211	Lavender-lt.
105	◇	∕	209	Lavender-dk.
110	■		208	Lavender-vy. dk.
158	△	∕	747	Sky Blue-vy. lt.
167	+		519	Sky Blue
975	+	∕	775	Baby Blue-vy. lt.
130	O	∕	809	Delft
131	X	∕	798	Delft-dk.
206	△	∕	955	Nile Green-lt.
203	U	∕	954	Nile Green
209	∕	∕	913	Nile Green-med.
205	◆		911	Emerald Green-med.
210	●		562	Jade-med.
885	·	∕	739	Tan-ultra vy. lt.
362	⁒	∕	437	Tan-lt.
881	−	∕	945	Peach Beige
347	∕	∕	402	Mahogany-vy. lt.
324	□		922	Copper-lt.
349	S	∕	301	Mahogany-med.
355	∴	∕	975	Golden Brown-dk.
397	−	∕	762	Pearl Gray-vy. lt.
399	□	∕	318	Steel Gray-lt.
400	◪		317	Pewter Gray
403	▲	∕	310	Black

Step 2: Backstitch (1 strand)

Anchor	DMC	Color
42	3350	Dusty Rose-dk. (ribbons, "Welcome" banner ends, pink flowers, pink saddle edge, heart on pole base, bunny's pink skirt)
110	208	Lavender-vy. dk. (lavender flowers, stripes in egg on bottom right)
132	797	Royal Blue (clouds, raindrops, blue flowers, bridle, blue on saddle, cinch, breastplate, crupper outline, bunny pants, bunny apron, sleeve, shoes)
210	562	Jade-med. (grass, trees, leaves, buds, stems, top bunny collars, stripes in egg on bottom left, small bunny's dress)
355	975	Golden Brown-dk. (banner, bunnies chicks, poles, scrollwork, Easter egg basket, yellow flowers, yellow on horse, wheel)
400	317	Pewter Gray (all else)

Step 3: Lazy Daisy Stitch (1 strand)

Anchor	DMC	Color
42	3350	Dusty Rose-dk. (saddle, cinch)
210	562	Jade-med. (vining on house)

Step 4: French Knot (1 strand)

Anchor	DMC	Color
349	301	Mahogany-med.
400	317	Pewter Gray

Up A Tree!

Models (see photo)

Cart (#1): Stitched on celery green Linda 27 over 2 threads, the finished design size is 2⅛" x 1½". The fabric was cut 8" x 7".

FABRICS	DESIGN SIZES
Aida 11	2⅝" x 1⅞"
Aida 14	2⅛" x 1⅜"
Aida 18	1⅝" x 1⅛"
Hardanger 22	1⅜" x ⅞"

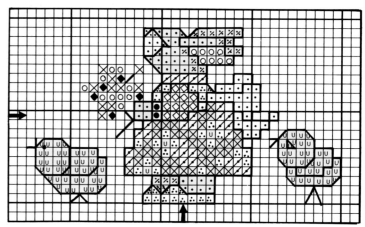

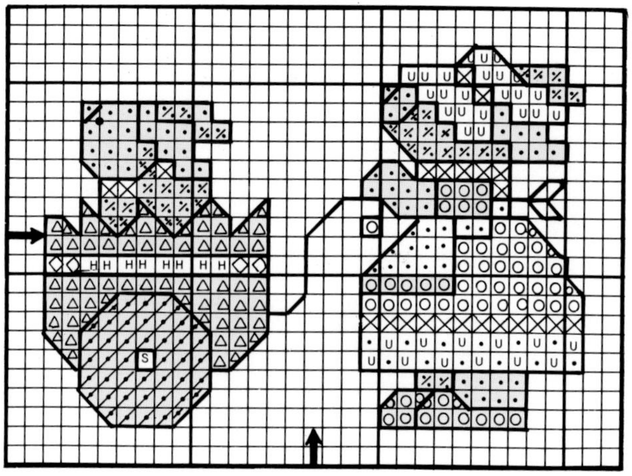

Stitch Count: 29 x 20 (Cart)

Bunny with chicks (#2): Stitched on celery green Linda 27 over 2 threads, the finished design size is 2⅝" x 1⅜". The fabric was cut 8" x 7".

FABRICS	DESIGN SIZES
Aida 11	3⅛" x 1¾"
Aida 14	2½" x 1⅜"
Aida 18	2" x 1"
Hardanger 22	1⅝" x ⅞"

Stitch Count: 35 x 19 (Bunny with chicks)

Bunny (#3): Stitched on ash rose Linda 27 over 2 threads, the finished design size is 1½" x 1½". The fabric was cut 8" x 7".

FABRICS	DESIGN SIZES
Aida 11	1⅞" x 1⅞"
Aida 14	1½" x 1½"
Aida 18	1⅛" x 1⅛"
Hardanger 22	1" x 1"

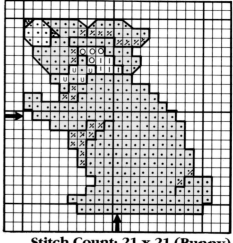

Stitch Count: 21 x 21 (Bunny)

Anchor   DMC (used for sample)

Step 1: Cross-stitch (2 strands)

1	·		⁄		White
301	U		U	744	Yellow-pale
10	⁒		⁄	352	Coral-lt.
48	I		⁄	818	Baby Pink
24	O		⁄	776	Pink-med.
76	X		⁄	962	Wild Rose-med.
86	∴		⁄	3608	Plum-vy. lt.
108	H		⁄	211	Lavender-lt.
105	◇		⁄	209	Lavender-dk.
158	△		⁄	747	Sky Blue-vy. lt.
159	+		⁄	775	Baby Blue-vy. lt.
130	O		⁄	809	Delft
131	X		⁄	798	Delft-dk.
206	△		⁄	955	Nile Green-lt.
203	U		U	954	Nile Green
209	⁄		⁄	913	Nile Green-med.
205	◆			911	Emerald Green-med.
210	●			562	Jade-med.
885	·		⁄	739	Tan-ultra vy. lt.
347	⁄		⁄	402	Mahogany-vy. lt.
349	S		s	301	Mahogany-med.
362	⁒		⁄	437	Tan-lt.
355	∷		⁄	975	Golden Brown-dk.

Step 2: Backstitch (1 strand)

42		3350	Dusty Rose-dk. (#1 bunny dress)
131		798	Delft-dk. (#1 bunny apron)
210		562	Jade-med. (#2 stems, #4 bunny dress)
349		301	Mahogany-med. (#4 bunnies)
355		975	Golden Brown-dk. (#1 bunnies and wheel, #2 bunny and chicks, #3 bunny, #5 chicks)
400		317	Pewter Gray (all else)

Step 3: French Knot (1 strand)

349	●	301	Mahogany-med.
400	■	317	Pewter Gray

Two bunnies (#4): Stitched on ash rose Linda 27 over 2 threads, the finished design size is 1¾" x 1⅜". The fabric was cut 8" x 7".

FABRICS	DESIGN SIZES
Aida 11	2⅛" x 1¾"
Aida 14	1¾" x 1⅜"
Aida 18	1⅜" x 1"
Hardanger 22	1⅛" x ⅞"

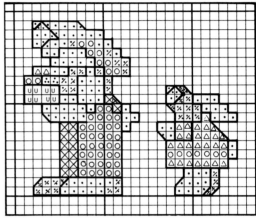

Stitch Count: 24 x 19 (Two bunnies)

Duck (#5): Stitched on ash rose Linda 27 over 2 threads, the finished design size is 2⅜" x 1½". The fabric was cut 8" x 7".

FABRICS	DESIGN SIZES
Aida 11	3" x 1⅞"
Aida 14	2¼" x 1⅜"
Aida 18	1¾" x 1⅛"
Hardanger 22	1½" x ⅞"

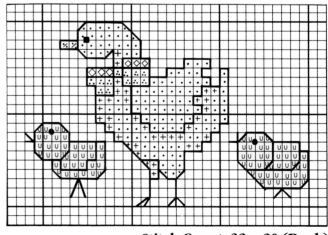

Stitch Count: 32 x 20 (Duck)

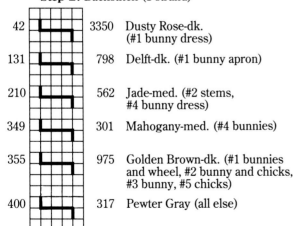

Materials (for five hearts)

Two completed designs on celery green
   Linda 27; matching thread
Three completed designs on ash rose Linda 27;
   matching thread
10" x 5" unstitched celery green Linda 27 piece
11½" x 10" unstitched ash rose Linda 27 piece
Purchased heart tree
6 yards of 1"-wide fabric strips (cut with pinking
   shears)
⅝ yard of ⅛"-wide mint green twisted rayon
   cording
1¼ yards of ⅛"-wide light blue twisted rayon
   cording
1¼ yards of ⅛"-wide cream twisted rayon
   cording
Polyester stuffing
Tracing paper
Dressmaker's pen

Directions

Seams are ¼".

1. Make pattern. Cut design pieces according to
pattern, centering design. Cut two green and
three rose unstitched Linda heart backs according
to pattern.

2. Stitch one heart front to one back of matching
color with right sides facing, leaving an opening.
Turn. Stuff moderately. Slipstitch opening closed.
Make two green and three rose hearts.

3. Cut cording into ⅝ yard lengths for each
heart. Knot ends of each cording length.
Whipstitch one end of one cording length
¼" below cleavage on back. Continue whip-
stitching cording around seam. End by making
a 2½"-deep hanger loop. Whipstitch remaining
knot to heart.

4. Wrap tree trunk and branches as desired with
fabric strips. Hang hearts on branches.

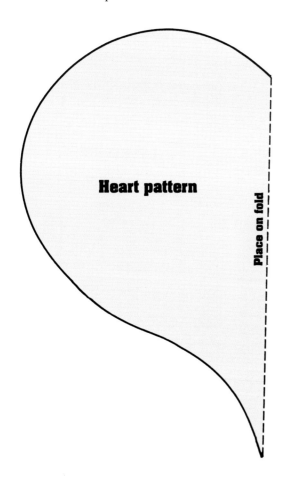

Heart pattern

Place on fold

Timely Welcome

Model (see photo)
The "Welcome" motif is from "March-Go-Round"
on pages 30–34. Stitched on white Linda 27 over
2 threads, the finished design size is 5⅞" x 3⅛".
The fabric was cut 12" x 10". Insert design in
clock according to manufacturer's instructions.
The stitch count is 80 x 42.

FABRICS	DESIGN SIZES
Aida 11	7¼" x 3⅞"
Aida 14	5¾" x 3"
Aida 18	4½" x 2⅜"
Hardanger 22	3⅝" x 1⅞"

48

Mother's May Fancy

Mother's May Fancy

921

921

921

921

Mother's May Fancy

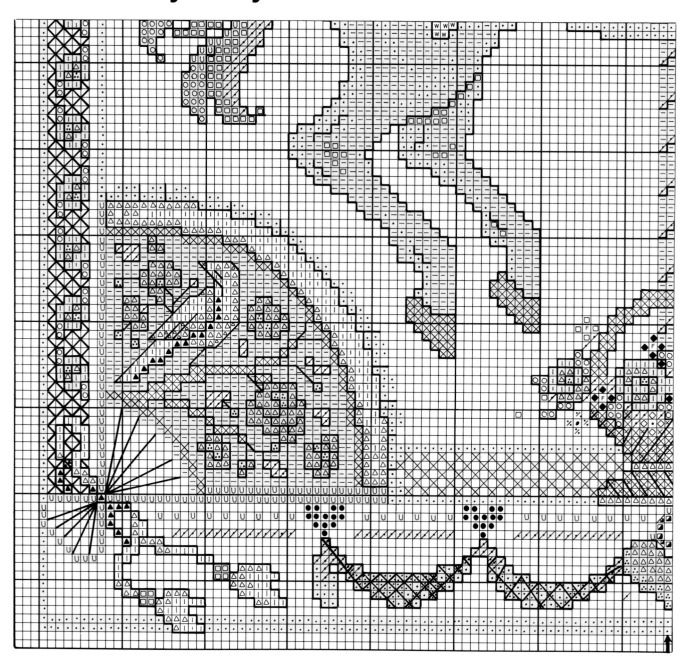

Stitch Count: 153 x 162

Mother's May Fancy

Model (see photo)
Stitched on black Aida 14, the finished design size is 10⅞" x 11⅝". The fabric was cut 17" x 18".

FABRICS	DESIGN SIZES
Aida 11	13⅞" x 14¾"
Aida 18	8½" x 9"
Hardanger 22	7" x 7⅜"

Anchor			DMC	(used for sample)
Step 1: Cross-stitch (3 strands)				
926	−	⁄		Ecru
300	•		745	Yellow-lt. pale
301	F		744	Yellow-pale
306	◪	◪	725	Topaz
48	I		818	Baby Pink
24	△		776	Pink-med.
27	∴		899	Rose-med.
13	●		349	Coral-dk.
85	□		3609	Plum-ultra lt.
86	⁒		3608	Plum-vy. lt.
105	◇		209	Lavender-dk.
110	◆		208	Lavender-vy. dk.
159	I	⁄	827	Blue-vy. lt.
160	△	◿	813	Blue-lt.
161	▲		826	Blue-med.
203	○		564	Jade-vy. lt.
210	⁄		562	Jade-med.
212	W	◹	561	Jade-vy. dk.
885	−	⁄	739	Tan-ultra vy. lt.
942	•	◿	738	Tan-vy. lt.
362	□		437	Tan-lt.
363	⁄		436	Tan
347	○		402	Mahogany-vy. lt.
324	U		922	Copper-lt.
349	✕		921	Copper
355	∴	◿	975	Golden Brown-dk.
376	+		842	Beige Brown-vy. lt.
378	✕		841	Beige Brown-lt.
379	P	◿	840	Beige Brown-med.
403	■	◿	310	Black

Step 2: Long Stitch (1 strand)

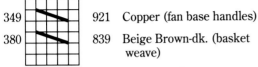

349	921 Copper (fan base handles)
380	839 Beige Brown-dk. (basket weave)

Step 3: Backstitch (1 strand)

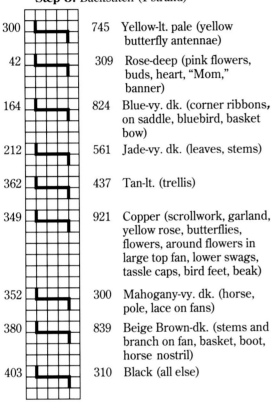

300	745 Yellow-lt. pale (yellow butterfly antennae)
42	309 Rose-deep (pink flowers, buds, heart, "Mom," banner)
164	824 Blue-vy. dk. (corner ribbons, on saddle, bluebird, basket bow)
212	561 Jade-vy. dk. (leaves, stems)
362	437 Tan-lt. (trellis)
349	921 Copper (scrollwork, garland, yellow rose, butterflies, flowers, around flowers in large top fan, lower swags, tassle caps, bird feet, beak)
352	300 Mahogany-vy. dk. (horse, pole, lace on fans)
380	839 Beige Brown-dk. (stems and branch on fan, basket, boot, horse nostril)
403	310 Black (all else)

A June Affair

A June Affair

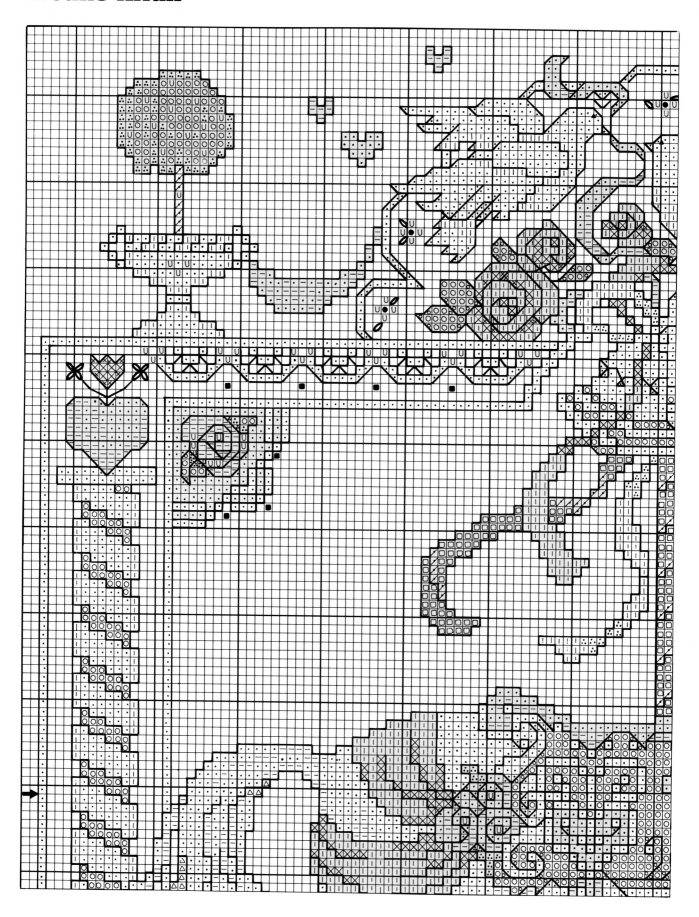

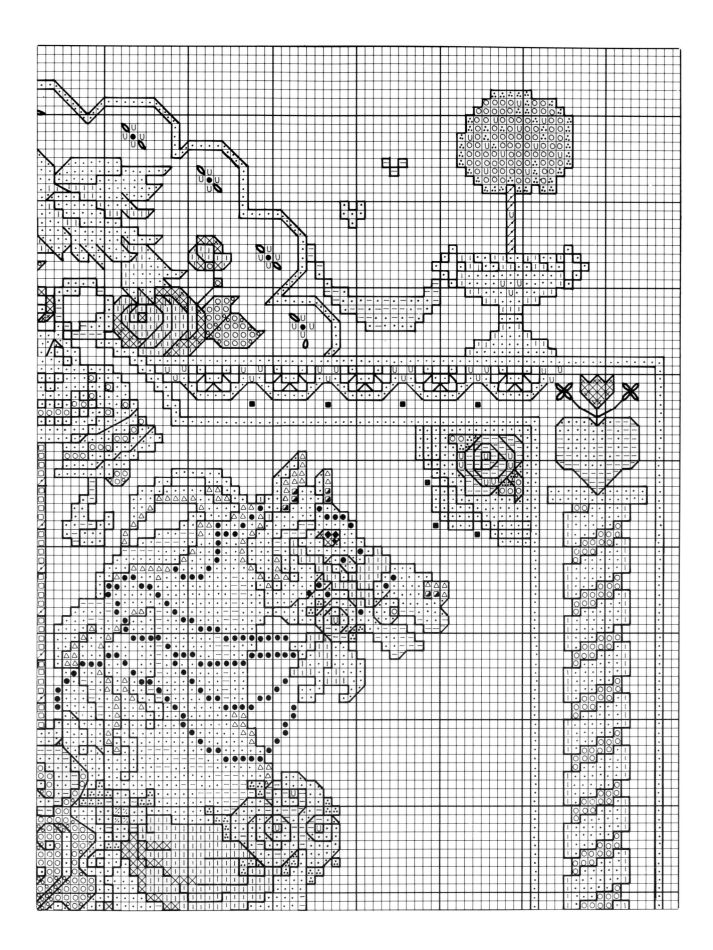

A June Affair

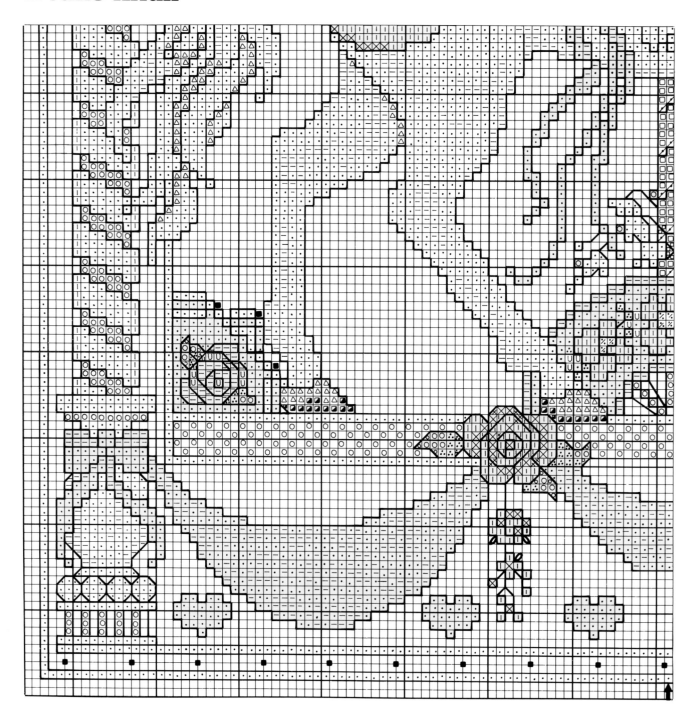

Stitch Count: 151 x 174

A June Affair

Model (see photo)
Stitched on white Linen 28 over 2 threads, the finished design size is 10¾" x 12⅜". The fabric was cut 17" x 19".

FABRICS	DESIGN SIZES
Aida 11	13¾" x 15⅞"
Aida 14	10¾" x 12⅜"
Aida 18	8⅜" x 9⅝"
Hardanger 22	6⅞" x 7⅞"

Anchor   **DMC (used for sample)**

Step 1: Cross-stitch (3 strands)

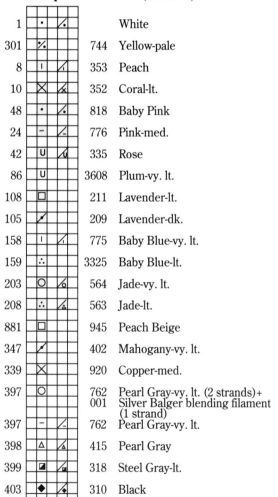

Anchor	DMC	Color
1		White
301	744	Yellow-pale
8	353	Peach
10	352	Coral-lt.
48	818	Baby Pink
24	776	Pink-med.
42	335	Rose
86	3608	Plum-vy. lt.
108	211	Lavender-lt.
105	209	Lavender-dk.
158	775	Baby Blue-vy. lt.
159	3325	Baby Blue-lt.
203	564	Jade-vy. lt.
208	563	Jade-lt.
881	945	Peach Beige
347	402	Mahogany-vy. lt.
339	920	Copper-med.
397	762 001	Pearl Gray-vy. lt. (2 strands)+ Silver Balger blending filament (1 strand)
397	762	Pearl Gray-vy. lt.
398	415	Pearl Gray
399	318	Steel Gray-lt.
403	310	Black

Step 2: Backstitch (1 strand)

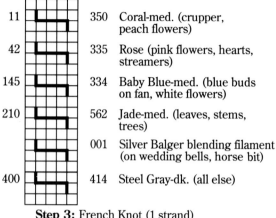

Anchor	DMC	Color
11	350	Coral-med. (crupper, peach flowers)
42	335	Rose (pink flowers, hearts, streamers)
145	334	Baby Blue-med. (blue buds on fan, white flowers)
210	562	Jade-med. (leaves, stems, trees)
	001	Silver Balger blending filament (on wedding bells, horse bit)
400	414	Steel Gray-dk. (all else)

Step 3: French Knot (1 strand)

Anchor	DMC	Color
403	310	Black

Step 4: Lazy Daisy Stitch (1 strand)

Anchor	DMC	Color
145	334	Baby Blue-med. (top corner hearts)
210	562	Jade-med. (leaves on pink flowers at top)

Step 5: Bows (1 strand)

Anchor	DMC	Color
42	335	Rose (Tie two bows with tails; attach one to each tree trunk)

Step 6: Pearls

●	small
■	large

Baby Fanfare

Model (see photo)
The fan motif is from "A June Affair" on pages 60–64. Stitched on Waste Canvas 14 on a purchased white baby dress over 2 threads, the finished design size is 2½" x 1¼" for each motif. Begin stitching first motif 1" from bottom edge of center dress front. Stitch to fill area as desired. Heavy lines on graph indicate placement of additional motifs. Add beads as desired (see photo). The stitch count is 35 x 17 for each motif.

FABRICS	DESIGN SIZES
Aida 11	3⅛" x 1½"
Aida 14	2½" x 1¼"
Aida 18	2" x 1¼"
Hardanger 22	1⅝" x ¾"

Scents Of Love

Model (see photo–page 59)
Stitched on pewter Murano 30 over 2 threads, the finished design size is 3½" x 1½". The fabric was cut 10" x 8".

FABRICS	DESIGN SIZES
Aida 11	4¾" x 2"
Aida 14	3¾" x 1⅝"
Aida 18	2⅞" x 1¼"
Hardanger 22	2⅜" x 1"

Anchor   **DMC (used for sample)**

Step 1: Cross-stitch (2 strands)

Anchor		DMC	
1			White
158		775	Baby Blue-vy. lt.

Step 2: Backstitch (1 strand)

399		318	Steel Gray-lt.

Step 3: French Knot (1 strand)

403		310	Black

Step 4: Ribbon Placement

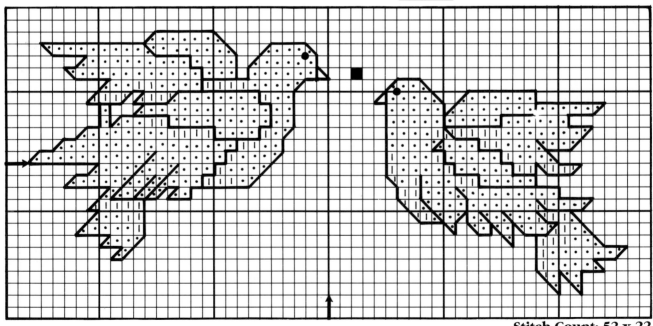

Stitch Count: 52 x 22

Materials

Completed design on pewter Murano 30
¼ yard of ¼"-wide white satin ribbon
9" x 7" mat board
Two 9½" x 7½" glass pieces
Purchased frame with an 8¾" x 6¾" window
Four ½"-round stick-on foam pads
1¼ yards of 1½"-wide molding
11½" x 9½" mat board
11½" x 9½" burgundy velvet piece
2 cups rose potpourri
Clear silicone caulking
Tracing paper
Dressmaker's pen
Staple gun
Tacky glue

Directions

1. Make pattern. Cut design piece according to pattern, paying careful attention to aligning edges with the grain of the fabric. Mark ½" inside and parallel to cut edge. Pull threads on top and side edges, making ½" deep fringe. To fringe bottom edge, unweave fabric for ½" and clip loose threads.

2. Fold ribbon length in half. Glue between doves' beaks as indicated on graph. Clip ends at an angle. Curl ribbon. Glue ends as desired (see photo).

3. Cut 8½" x 6½" window from center of 9" x 7" mat board, leaving a ½" frame on all sides. Place mat board frame and design piece on top of one glass piece, positioning design in lower left corner (see photo). Glue mat board and design piece to glass. Use small points of glue on design piece so glue will not bleed through fabric. Set aside to dry.

4. Secure remaining piece of glass into frame with silicone caulking. Place design piece glass in frame so mat board and design are sandwiched between glass pieces. Secure with holders on back of frame. Stick one small foam pad to each back corner of frame.

5. Cut molding into two 11½" lengths and two 9½" lengths. Miter corners, making front face of molding the side of the box (Diagram A). This will make the rabbet the top of the box so design piece frame will fit into recess (Diagrams B and C). Construct molding frame to measure slightly larger than outside edges of design piece frame. Secure corners.

6. Glue velvet to large mat board. Staple mat board to back of molding frame, velvet side up.

7. Place potpourri in molding box. Cover with design frame.

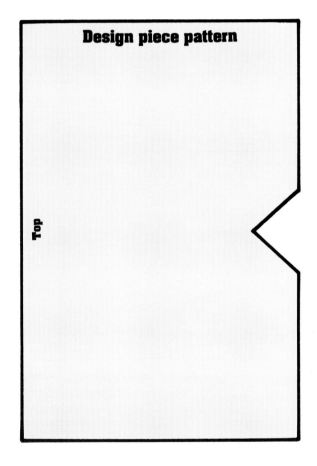

Design piece pattern

Top

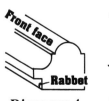

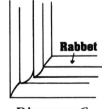

Diagram A   *Diagram B*   *Diagram C*

Dandy July Patriot

Dandy July Patriot

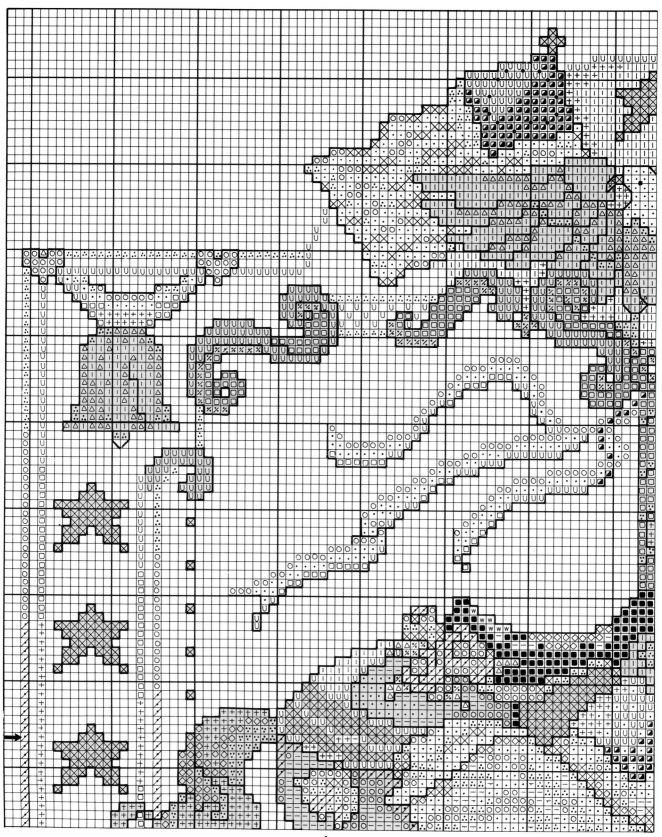

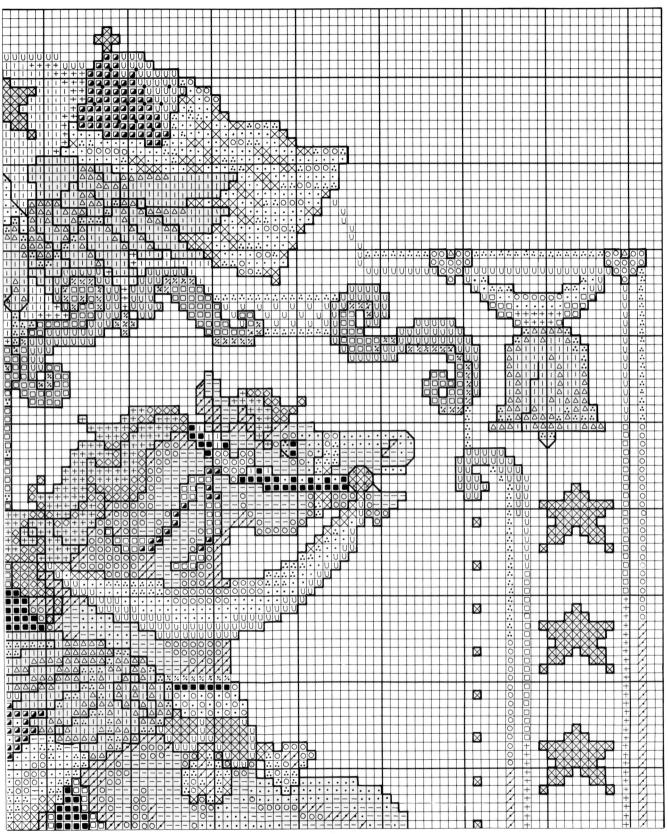

Dandy July Patriot

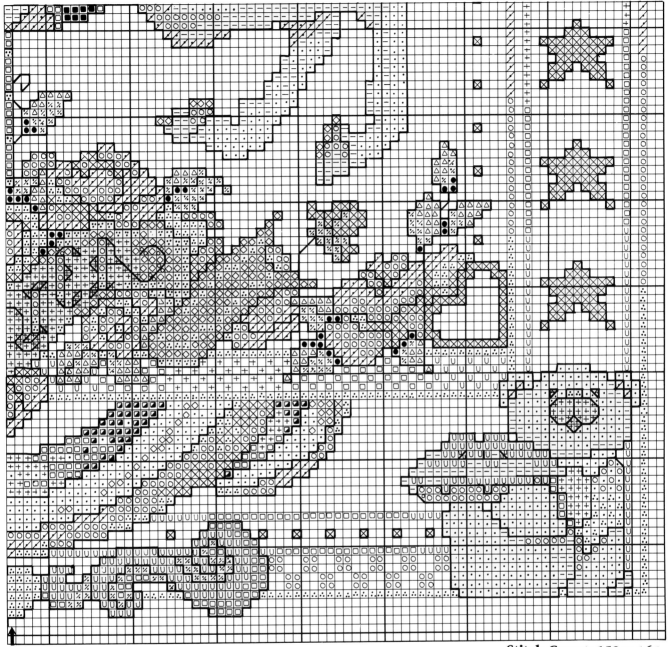

Stitch Count: 153 x 165

Dandy July Patriot

Model (see photo)
Stitched on white Dublin Linen 25 over
2 threads, the finished design size is
12¼" x 13¼". The fabric was cut 19" x 20".

FABRICS	DESIGN SIZES
Aida 11	13⅞" x 15"
Aida 14	10⅞" x 11¾"
Aida 18	8½" x 9⅛"
Hardanger 22	7" x 7½"

Anchor			DMC (used for sample)	
	Step 1: Cross-stitch (2 strands)			
1	·	⁄		White
886	U		3047	Yellow Beige-lt.
891	□		676	Old Gold-lt.
307	⅄		783	Christmas Gold
306	⊠		725	Topaz
881	·	⁄	945	Peach Beige
347	−	⁄	402	Mahogany-vy. lt.
324	O		922	Copper-lt.
339	⁄		921	Copper
330	⁄		947	Burnt Orange
46	O	⁄	666	Christmas Red-bright
22	∴		816	Garnet
44	⊠		814	Garnet-dk.
158	ǀ	⁄	775	Baby Blue-vy. lt.
130	+	⁄	809	Delft
131	□		798	Delft-dk.
132	U		797	Royal Blue
134	◪		820	Royal Blue-vy. dk.
265	△		3348	Yellow Green-lt.
266	⅄		3347	Yellow Green-med.
268	●		3345	Hunter Green-dk.
885	+	⁄	739	Tan-ultra vy. lt.
362	◇		437	Tan-lt.
309	∴		435	Brown-vy. lt.
376	ǀ	⁄	842	Beige Brown-vy. lt.
378	△		841	Beige Brown-lt.
380	∴	⁄	839	Beige Brown-dk.
397	−		762	Pearl Gray-vy. lt.
399	◇		318	Steel Gray-lt.
401	W		413	Pewter Gray-dk.
403	■		310	Black

Step 2: Backstitch (1 strand)

339	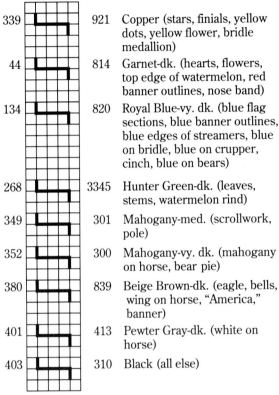	921	Copper (stars, finials, yellow dots, yellow flower, bridle medallion)
44		814	Garnet-dk. (hearts, flowers, top edge of watermelon, red banner outlines, nose band)
134		820	Royal Blue-vy. dk. (blue flag sections, blue banner outlines, blue edges of streamers, blue on bridle, blue on crupper, cinch, blue on bears)
268		3345	Hunter Green-dk. (leaves, stems, watermelon rind)
349		301	Mahogany-med. (scrollwork, pole)
352		300	Mahogany-vy. dk. (mahogany on horse, bear pie)
380		839	Beige Brown-dk. (eagle, bells, wing on horse, "America," banner)
401		413	Pewter Gray-dk. (white on horse)
403		310	Black (all else)

Step 3: French Knot (1 strand)

1	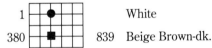		White
380		839	Beige Brown-dk.

August In Santa Fe

August In Santa Fe

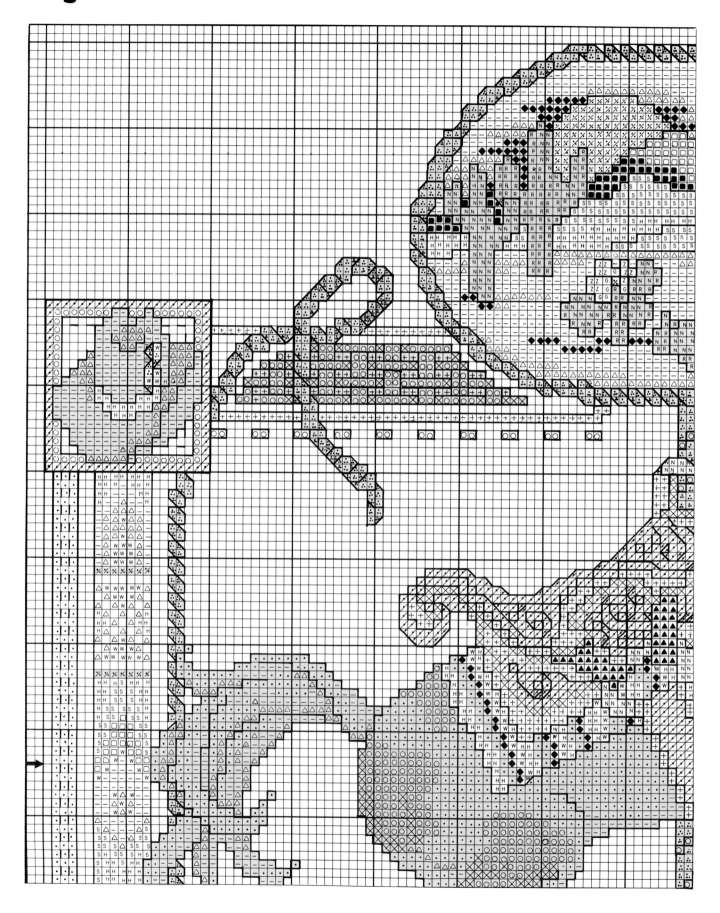

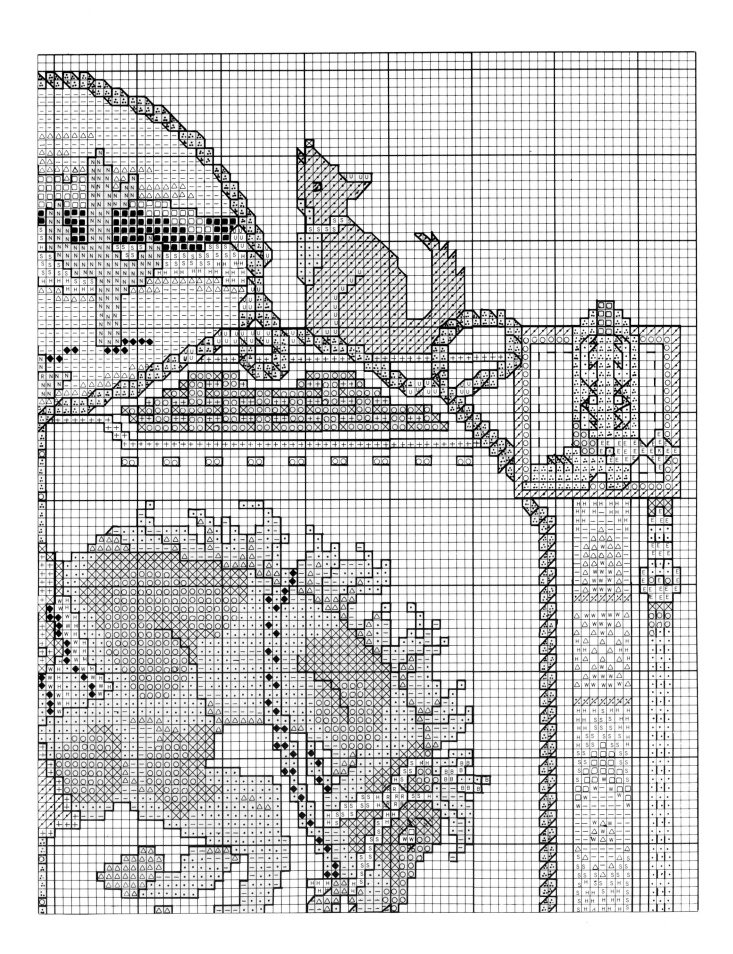

August In Santa Fe

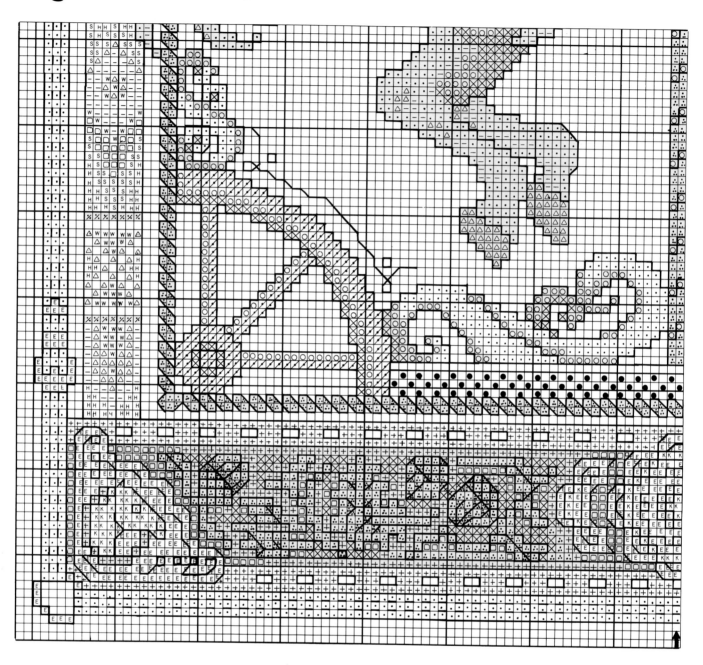

Stitch Count: 155 x 168

August In Santa Fe

Model (see photo)

Stitched on Fiddlers Lite 14, the finished design size is 11⅛" x 12". The fabric was cut 18" x 18".

FABRICS	DESIGN SIZES
Aida 11	14⅛" x 15¼"
Aida 14	11⅛" x 12"
Aida 18	8⅝" x 9⅜"
Hardanger 22	7" x 7⅝"

Anchor			DMC (used for sample)	
Step 1: Cross-stitch (2 strands)				
1	·	⁄		White
301	⁒		744	Yellow-pale
8	–	⁄	353	Peach
10	△	⁄	352	Coral-lt.
11	◆		351	Coral
13	∴	⁄	349	Coral-dk.
75	Z		604	Cranberry-lt.
76	G		603	Cranberry
95	□		554	Violet-lt.
98	■		553	Violet-med.
160	S	⁄	3761	Sky Blue-lt.
433	H	⁄	996	Electric Blue-med.
209	N		913	Nile Green-med.
210	R		562	Jade-med.
188	⁒		943	Aquamarine-med.
885	·		739	Tan-ultra vy. lt.
942	∴	⁄	738	Tan-vy. lt.
363	U	⁄	436	Tan
371	▲		433	Brown-med.
347	O		402	Mahogany-vy. lt.
324	✕		922	Copper-lt.
339	+	⁄	920	Copper-med.
341	□	⁄	918	Red Copper-dk.
376	⁄	⁄	842	Beige Brown-vy. lt.
378	+	⁄	841	Beige Brown-lt.
379	O	⁄	840	Beige Brown-med.
380	✕		839	Beige Brown-dk.
381	●		838	Beige Brown-vy. dk.
900	⁄	⁄	3023	Brown Gray-lt.
8581	U	⁄	3022	Brown Gray-med.
397	–	⁄	762	Pearl Gray-vy. lt.
399	△		318	Steel Gray-lt.
400	B		317	Pewter Gray
403	W	⁄	310	Black

| | N | | | | 001P | Silver Balger cable (6 strands) |

| | | R | ▟ | | 002P | Gold Balger cable (6 strands) |

397 | | E | ⟋Ɇ | | ⌐762 | Pearl Gray-vy. lt. (1 strand)+
| | | | | | ⌐001P | Silver Balger cable (3 strands) |

301 | | K | ⟋K | | ⌐744 | Yellow-pale (1 strand)+
| | | | | | ⌐002P | Gold Balger cable (3 strands) |

Step 2: Backstitch (1 strand)

11   351   Coral (sun)

76   603   Cranberry (cactus flower)

98   553   Violet-med. (violet mountains)

433   996   Electric Blue-med. (blue mountains, coyote collar)

212   561   Jade-vy. dk. (cacti)

371   433   Brown-med. (rope, belt borders)

341   918   Red Copper-dk. (top woven sections, scrollwork, leaves, acorns, corner horse heads)

380   839   Beige Brown-dk. (top corner squares, bands, dashes, coyote, saddle, cinch, line under scrollwork, wheels and trim, bottom dash outline)

400   317   Pewter Gray (cowboy hat and band, horse)

401   413   Pewter Gray-dk. (boot, silver buckles, saddle horn tip, silver saddle trim, bottom corners, center medallions)

403   310   Black (all else)

Cowboy Camp Lamp

Model (see photo)
Stitched on natural Super Linen 27 over
2 threads, the finished design size is 1½" x 1¾"
for each motif. See Step 1 of Directions before
cutting and stitching fabric.

FABRICS	DESIGN SIZES
Aida 11	1⅞" x 2⅛"
Aida 14	1⅜" x 1⅝"
Aida 18	1⅛" x 1¼"
Hardanger 22	⅞" x 1"

Materials
Two completed designs on natural Super
 Linen 27; matching thread
5" x 12" hurricane lamp
Candy to fill chimney

Directions
Seams are ¼".

1. Before stitching design, measure around lamp
for band placement and add 6" for horizontal
measurement. Add 6" to vertical measurement
of motif. Cut two unstitched fabric strips to
match measurements; stitch two. Center
design vertically and begin stitching first
motif 2½" from one short end of one strip.

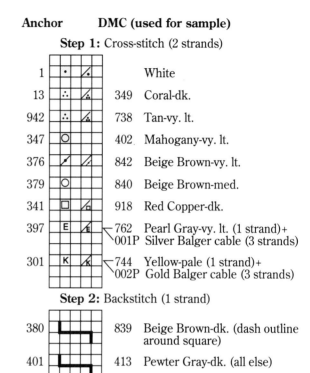

Anchor			DMC (used for sample)	
Step 1: Cross-stitch (2 strands)				
1	·	⁄		White
13	∴	⁄	349	Coral-dk.
942	∴	⁄	738	Tan-vy. lt.
347	O		402	Mahogany-vy. lt.
376	⁄	⁄	842	Beige Brown-vy. lt.
379	O		840	Beige Brown-med.
341	□	⁄	918	Red Copper-dk.
397	E	E	762	Pearl Gray-vy. lt. (1 strand)+
			001P	Silver Balger cable (3 strands)
301	K	K	744	Yellow-pale (1 strand)+
			002P	Gold Balger cable (3 strands)
Step 2: Backstitch (1 strand)				
380			839	Beige Brown-dk. (dash outline around square)
401			413	Pewter Gray-dk. (all else)

Stitch repeats to fill horizontally, leaving 2½"
unstitched at opposite end. Heavy lines on graph
indicate placement of additional motifs. Measure
1¼" above and below design; trim fabric.
Measure ¾" from each end motif; trim fabric.

3. With right sides facing and long raw
edges aligned, fold strip in half. Stitch
long edge to make tube. Turn right side
out. Position seam in center back and
press.

4. Wrap band around lamp. Fold in seam
allowance on one end of band. Insert raw
edge of other end into folded end. Slipstitch ends together.

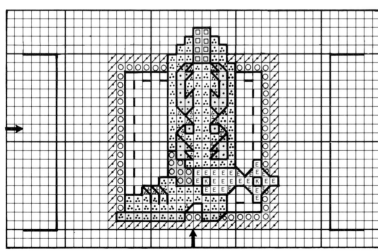

Stitch Count: 20 x 23 (each motif)

A Whirlwind September

A Whirlwind September

A Whirlwind September

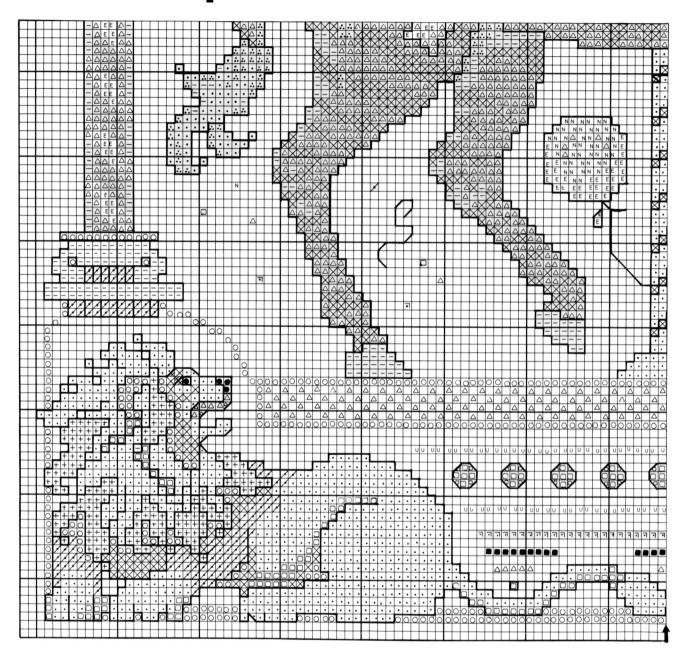

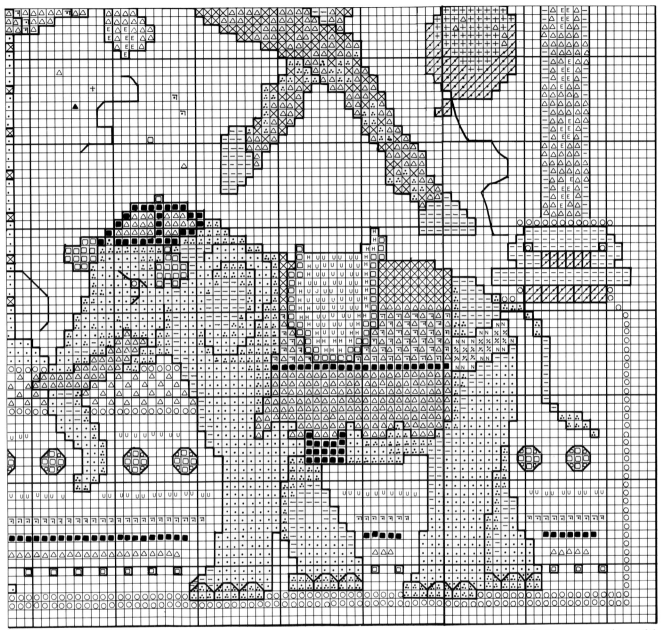

Stitch Count: 154 x 166

A Whirlwind September

Model (see photo)

Stitched on antique white Aida 14, the finished design size is 11" x 11⅞". The fabric was cut 17" x 18".

FABRICS	DESIGN SIZES
Aida 11	14" x 15⅛"
Aida 18	8½" x 9¼"
Hardanger 22	7" x 7½"

Anchor			DMC (used for sample)	
			Step 1: Cross-stitch (2 strands)	
1	△	◿		White
300	⁒		745	Yellow-lt. pale
297	☐	◸	743	Yellow-med.
316	N		740	Tangerine
330	E	◿	947	Burnt Orange
46	△	◿	666	Christmas Red-bright
22	⁒		816	Garnet
85	+		3609	Plum-ultra lt.
86	╱		3608	Plum-vy. lt.
105	◩	◿	209	Lavender-dk.
130	◇		799	Delft-med.
131	◆		798	Delft-dk.
433	▲	◿	996	Electric Blue-med.
185	U		964	Seagreen-lt.
186	Z		959	Seagreen-med.
187	H		958	Seagreen-dk.
256	◩		704	Chartreuse-bright
239	■		702	Kelly Green
885	+		739	Tan-ultra vy. lt.
942	·		738	Tan-vy. lt.
362	☐	◸	437	Tan-lt.
881	–		945	Peach Beige
347	╱	◿	402	Mahogany-vy. lt.
324	✕	◿	922	Copper-lt.
349	○		921	Copper
352	∴	◿	300	Mahogany-vy. dk.
381	●	◿	838	Beige Brown-vy. dk.
397	·	◿	762	Pearl Gray-vy. lt.
398	–	◿	415	Pearl Gray
399	∴	◿	318	Steel Gray-lt.
400	○	◿	317	Pewter Gray
403	✕		310	Black

Step 2: Backstitch (1 strand)

46	666	Christmas Red-bright (red stripe on small poles, four red confetti strings)
85	3609	Plum-ultra lt. (one plum confetti string)
105	209	Lavender-dk. (one lavender confetti string)
186	959	Seagreen-med. (one seagreen confetti string)
131	798	Delft-dk. (one delft confetti string)
433	996	Electric Blue-med. (one blue confetti string)
256	704	Chartreuse-bright (one chartreuse confetti string)
352	300	Mahogany-vy. dk. (tiger, lions, giraffe, carousel pole, yellow dots, circles and streamers, yellow and orange balloon, yellow plume and medallions on bridle, tops and bottoms of side poles)
401	413	Pewter Gray-dk. (all else)

Step 3: French Knot (1 strand)

352	300	Mahogany-vy.dk.

Haunted October Nights

Haunted October Nights

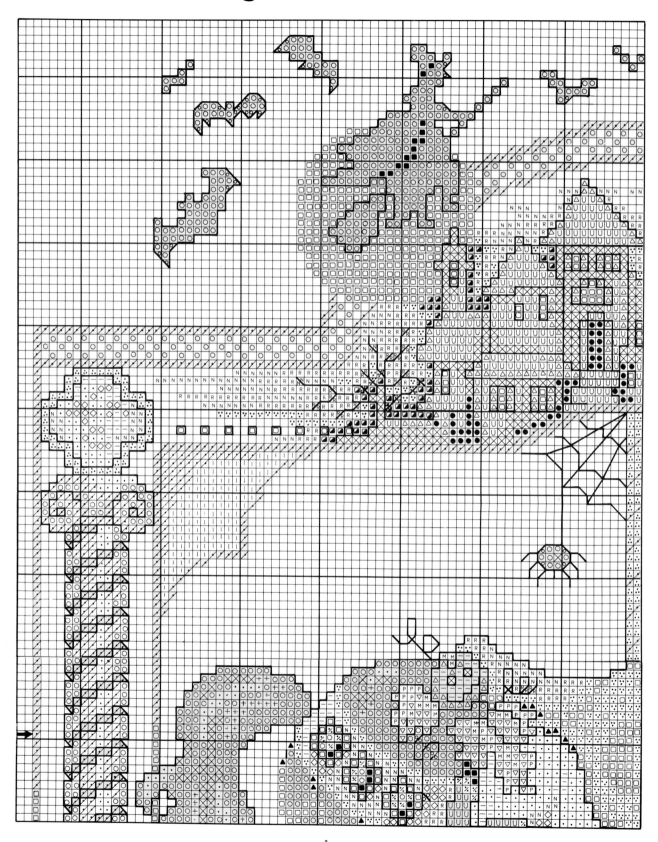

Haunted October Nights

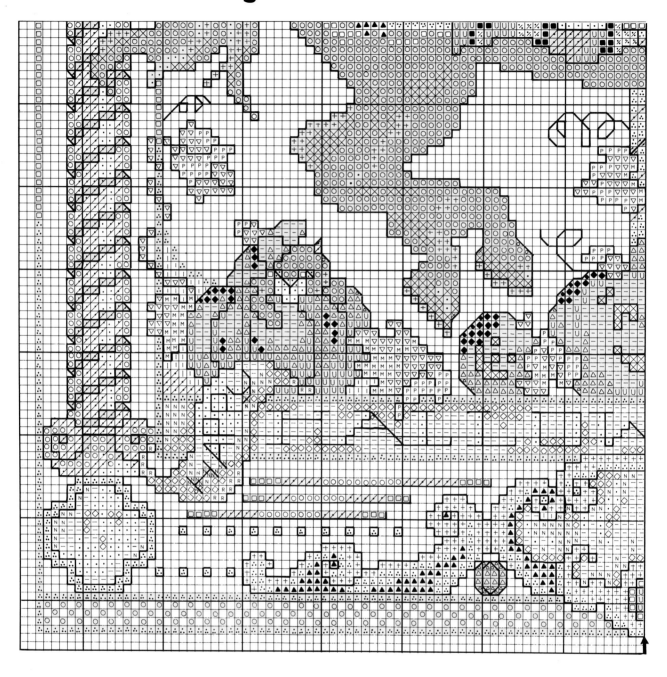

Stitch Count: 152 x 169

Haunted October Nights

Model (see photo)
Stitched on natural Linen 28 over 2 threads, the finished design size is 10⅞" x 12⅛". The fabric was cut 17" x 19".

FABRICS	DESIGN SIZES
Aida 11	13⅞" x 15⅜"
Aida 14	10⅞" x 12⅛"
Aida 18	8½" x 9⅜"
Hardanger 22	6⅞" x 7⅝"

Anchor   **DMC (used for sample)**

Step 1: Cross-stitch (2 strands)

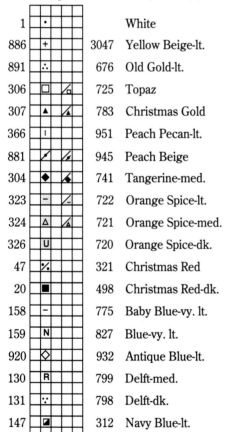

Anchor	DMC	Color
1		White
886	3047	Yellow Beige-lt.
891	676	Old Gold-lt.
306	725	Topaz
307	783	Christmas Gold
366	951	Peach Pecan-lt.
881	945	Peach Beige
304	741	Tangerine-med.
323	722	Orange Spice-lt.
324	721	Orange Spice-med.
326	720	Orange Spice-dk.
47	321	Christmas Red
20	498	Christmas Red-dk.
158	775	Baby Blue-vy. lt.
159	827	Blue-vy. lt.
920	932	Antique Blue-lt.
130	799	Delft-med.
131	798	Delft-dk.
147	312	Navy Blue-lt.
265	3348	Yellow Green-lt.
266	3347	Yellow Green-med.
268	3345	Hunter Green-dk.
347	402	Mahogany-vy. lt.
324	922	Copper-lt.
349	301	Mahogany-med.
351	400	Mahogany-dk.
362	437	Tan-lt.
363	436	Tan
370	434	Brown-lt.
357	801	Coffee Brown-dk.
381	938	Coffee Brown-ultra dk.
398	415	Pearl Gray
400	414	Steel Gray-dk.
401	413	Pewter Gray-dk.
403	310	Black

Step 2: Backstitch (1 strand)

Anchor	DMC	Color
20	498	Christmas Red-dk. (bridle, tassels, medallions on crupper)
147	312	Navy Blue-lt. (banner, saddle, "Happy Halloween," crupper end near tail)
268	3345	Hunter Green-dk. (vines and leaves on pumpkins)
349	301	Mahogany-med. (outer border, carousel pole, pumpkins)
381	938	Coffee Brown-ultra dk. (house, trees, ghost eyes, pumpkin faces)
401	413	Pewter Gray-dk. (spider web)
403	310	Black (all else)

Little Pumpkin Goblin

Models (see photo)

Pajamas: Stitched with Waste Canvas 14 on purchased white two-piece baby pajamas, the finished design size is 4⅜" x 1⅞" for pajama top motif and 1⅝" x 1⅝" for pajama pant motif. For pajama top motif, stitch treat bag motif, omitting top leaf cluster.

Pajama top motif

FABRICS	DESIGN SIZES
Aida 11	5½" x 2⅜"
Aida 14	4⅜" x 1⅞"
Aida 18	3⅜" x 1½"
Hardanger 22	2¾" x 1⅛"

Pajama pant motif

FABRICS	DESIGN SIZES
Aida 11	2" x 2"
Aida 14	1⅝" x 1⅝"
Aida 18	1¼" x ¼"
Hardanger 22	1" x 1"

Treat bag: Stitched on black Aida 14, the finished design size is 4⅜" x 2⅞". The fabric was cut 11" x 9".

FABRICS	DESIGN SIZES
Aida 11	5½" x 3¾"
Aida 18	3⅜" x 2¼"
Hardanger 22	2¾" x 1⅞"

Materials (for treat bag)

Completed design on black Aida 14; matching thread

7" x 6" unstitched black Aida 14 piece for back

Two 8" x 6" black chintz pieces for lining

½ yard of ⅝"-wide black satin ribbon

Directions

Seams are ¼".

1. Cut design piece to 7" x 6" with bottom of design 1¾" above bottom edge for front. Cut two 9" lengths from ribbon for handles.

2. With right sides facing, stitch front to back, leaving top edge open. Fold with side and bottom seam aligned and stitch 1" from each corner (Diagram A). Turn. Repeat for lining. Do not turn.

3. With raw edges aligned, center and pin handle ends over sides of bag (Diagram B).

4. Slide lining over design piece with right sides facing and side seams matching. Stitch top raw edge, catching handle ends in seam and leaving an opening. Turn. Slipstitch opening closed. Fold lining inside bag.

Stitch Count: 22 x 22 (Pajama pant motif)

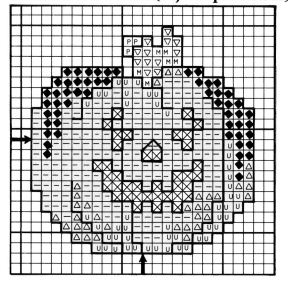

Diagram A

Diagram B

Anchor			DMC (used for sample)	

Step 1: Cross-stitch (2 strands)

Anchor			DMC	
307	▲	◿	783	Christmas Gold
304	◆	◆	741	Tangerine-med.
323	−	◹	722	Orange Spice-lt.
324	△	◿	721	Orange Spice-med.
326	U		720	Orange Spice-dk.
265	P		3348	Yellow Green-lt.
266	▽		3347	Yellow Green-med.
268	M		3345	Hunter Green-dk.
357	✕		801	Coffee Brown-dk.

Step 2: Backstitch (1 strand)

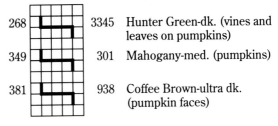

Anchor		DMC	
268		3345	Hunter Green-dk. (vines and leaves on pumpkins)
349		301	Mahogany-med. (pumpkins)
381		938	Coffee Brown-ultra dk. (pumpkin faces)

Stitch Count: 61 x 26 (Pajama top motif)   **Stitch Count: 61 x 41 (Treat bag)**

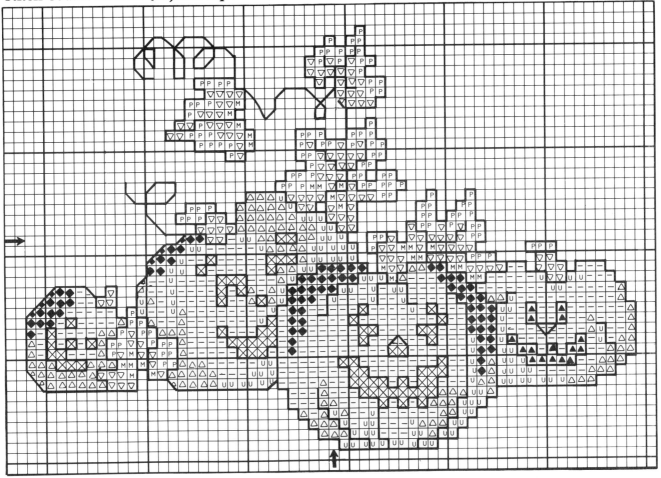

November O'Plenty

November O'Plenty

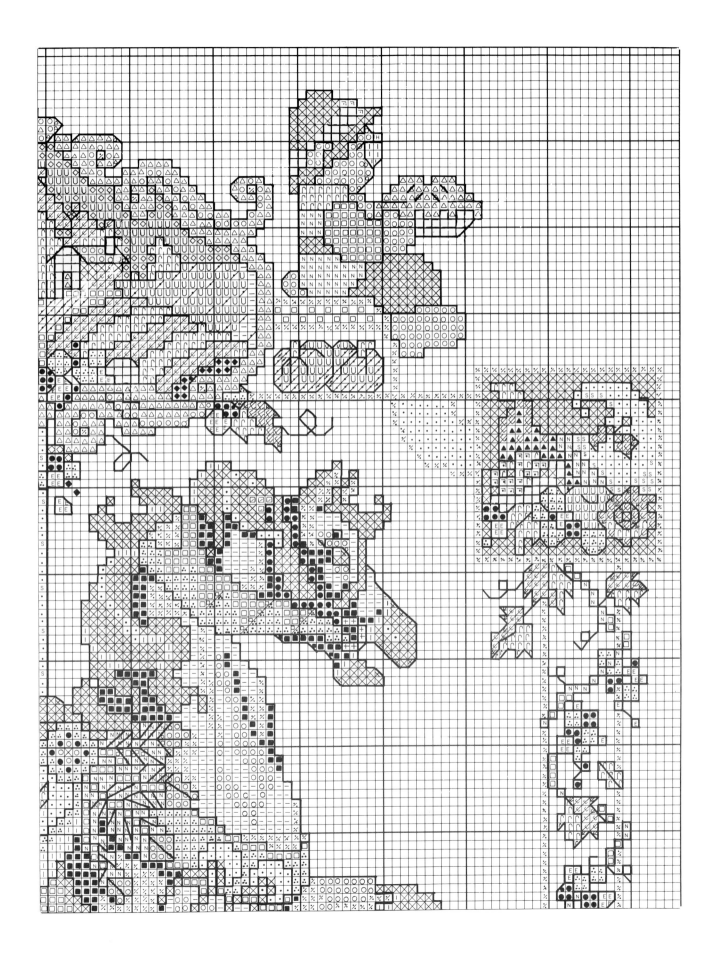

November O'Plenty

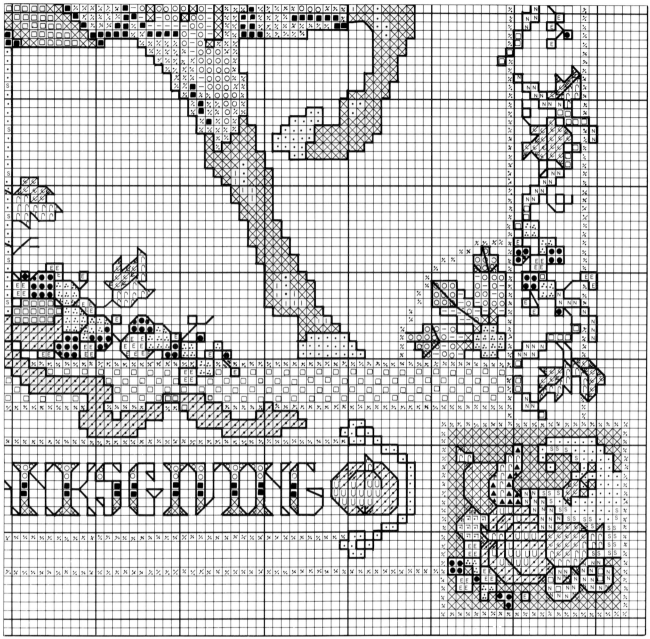

Stitch Count: 151 x 169

November O'Plenty

Model (see photo)
Stitched on tea-dyed Linen 28 over 2 threads, the finished design size is 10¾" x 12⅛". The fabric was cut 17" x 18".

FABRICS	DESIGN SIZES
Aida 11	13¾" x 15⅜"
Aida 14	10¾" x 12⅛"
Aida 18	8⅜" x 9⅜"
Hardanger 22	6⅞" x 7⅝"

Anchor **DMC (used for sample)**

Step 1: Cross-stitch (2 strands)

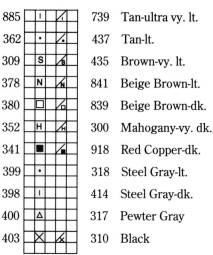

Anchor			DMC	Color
1	O			White
301	◙		744	Yellow-pale
297	+		743	Yellow-med.
881	△		945	Peach Beige
323	U		722	Orange Spice-lt.
326	/		721	Orange Spice-med.
347	O		402	Mahogany-vy. lt.
324	−		922	Copper-lt.
349	%		921	Copper
11			350	Coral-med.
47	X		321	Christmas Red
95	∴		554	Violet-lt.
87	E		3607	Plum-lt.
99	●		552	Violet-dk.
158	U		775	Baby Blue-vy. lt.
159	◇		3325	Baby Blue-lt.
167	∴		3766	Peacock Blue-lt.
208	/		563	Jade-lt.
210	□		562	Jade-med.
265			3348	Yellow Green-lt.
266	ſ		3347	Yellow Green-med.
257	◆		3346	Hunter Green
268	▲		3345	Hunter Green-dk.

Anchor			DMC	Color
885	I		739	Tan-ultra vy. lt.
362	•		437	Tan-lt.
309	S		435	Brown-vy. lt.
378	N		841	Beige Brown-lt.
380	□		839	Beige Brown-dk.
352	H		300	Mahogany-vy. dk.
341	■		918	Red Copper-dk.
399	•		318	Steel Gray-lt.
398	I		414	Steel Gray-dk.
400	△		317	Pewter Gray
403	X		310	Black

Step 2: Backstitch (1 strand)

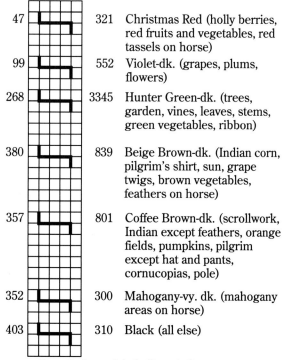

Anchor	DMC	Color
47	321	Christmas Red (holly berries, red fruits and vegetables, red tassels on horse)
99	552	Violet-dk. (grapes, plums, flowers)
268	3345	Hunter Green-dk. (trees, garden, vines, leaves, stems, green vegetables, ribbon)
380	839	Beige Brown-dk. (Indian corn, pilgrim's shirt, sun, grape twigs, brown vegetables, feathers on horse)
357	801	Coffee Brown-dk. (scrollwork, Indian except feathers, orange fields, pumpkins, pilgrim except hat and pants, cornucopias, pole)
352	300	Mahogany-vy. dk. (mahogany areas on horse)
403	310	Black (all else)

Step 3: Long Stitch (1 strand)

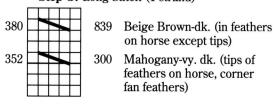

Anchor	DMC	Color
380	839	Beige Brown-dk. (in feathers on horse except tips)
352	300	Mahogany-vy. dk. (tips of feathers on horse, corner fan feathers)

Autumn Accents

Model (see photo)

Place mat design strip: Stitched on black Dublin Linen 25 over 2 threads, the finished design size is 1⅞" x 3⅞" for each motif. The fabric was cut 8" x 16". See Step 1 of Directions to stitch.

Napkin ring motif: Stitched on black Dublin Linen 25 over 2 threads, the finished design size is 1⅞" x 3⅞" for each motif. The fabric was cut 8" x 10". See Step 1 of Directions to stitch.

FABRICS	DESIGN SIZES
Aida 11	2⅛" x 4½"
Aida 14	1⅝" x 3½"
Aida 18	1¼" x 2¾"
Hardanger 22	1" x 2¼"

Anchor   **DMC (used for sample)**

Step 1: Cross-stitch (2 strands)

Anchor			DMC	
301			744	Yellow-pale
323	U		722	Orange Spice-lt.
324			721	Orange Spice-med.
349			921	Copper
11			350	Coral-med.
47	X		321	Christmas Red
95			554	Violet-lt.
87	E		3607	Plum-lt.
99	●		552	Violet-dk.
265			3348	Yellow Green-lt.
266	r		3347	Yellow Green-med.
268	▲		3345	Hunter Green-dk.
362	·		437	Tan-lt.
309	S		435	Brown-vy. lt.
378	N		841	Beige Brown-lt.
380	□		839	Beige Brown-dk.

Step 2: Backstitch (1 strand)

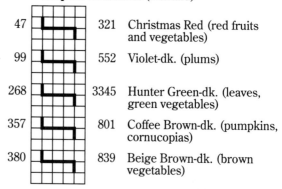

		DMC	
47		321	Christmas Red (red fruits and vegetables)
99		552	Violet-dk. (plums)
268		3345	Hunter Green-dk. (leaves, green vegetables)
357		801	Coffee Brown-dk. (pumpkins, cornucopias)
380		839	Beige Brown-dk. (brown vegetables)

Materials (for one napkin ring and napkin)
Completed design on black Dublin Linen 25; matching thread
16" square of burnt orange chintz; matching thread

Directions
Seams are ¼".

1. Center design vertically and begin stitching first motif. Stitch repeats to fill ring. Heavy lines on graph indicate placement of additional motifs. Measure 1¾" on each side of design; trim fabric. Measure 1⅛" from each end motif; trim fabric.

2. With right sides facing and long raw edges aligned, fold napkin ring in half. Stitch long edge to make tube. Turn right side out. Position seam in center back and press.

3. Fold in seam allowance on one end of band. Insert raw edge of other end into folded end. Slip-stitch ends together.

4. For napkin, hem edges; press. Place napkin in napkin ring.

Materials (for one place mat)

Completed design on black Dublin Linen 25; matching thread
½ yard of burnt orange chintz; matching thread
12½" x 18" fleece piece

Directions

Seams are ¼".

1. Center and begin stitching first motif pair. Stitch motifs to fill length. Heavy lines on graph indicate placement of additional motifs. Measure ½" on each side of design; trim fabric. Measure 2" from each end motif; trim fabric.

2. Cut one 3¼" x 12½" chintz strip and one 13" x 12½" chintz piece. Cut one 18" x 12½" chintz back. Also cut 1¾"-wide bias strips, piecing as needed to make 1¾ yards for binding.

3. For front, stitch one long edge of design strip to one long edge of 3¼" x 12½" chintz strip with right sides facing. Repeat with remaining long edge of design strip and 13" x 12½" chintz piece. Press flat.

4. Layer back (wrong side up), fleece and front (right side up) with raw edges aligned; stitch. Trim seam allowance. With right sides facing and raw edges aligned, stitch binding to front, over stitching line. Stitch to, but not through, seam allowance; backstitch (Diagram A). Fold bias at a 90° angle to stitched edge and turn corner. Resume stitching, meeting the backstitch at seam allowance (Diagram A). Fold bias to back, turning under seam allowance. Slipstitch, covering stitch line of binding and mitering each corner on both sides of fabric.

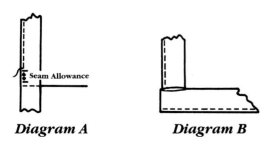

Diagram A   Diagram B

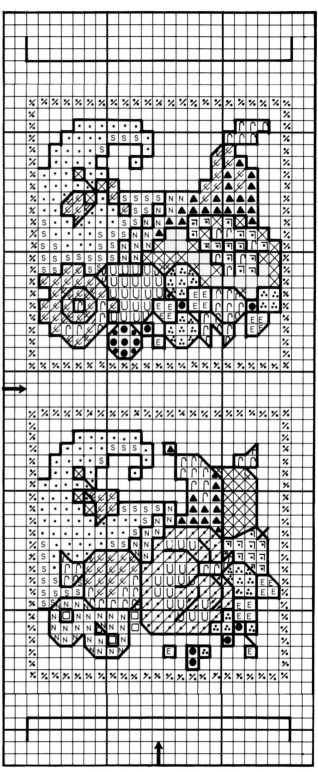

Stitch Count: 23 x 49 (each motif)

December Delights

December Delights

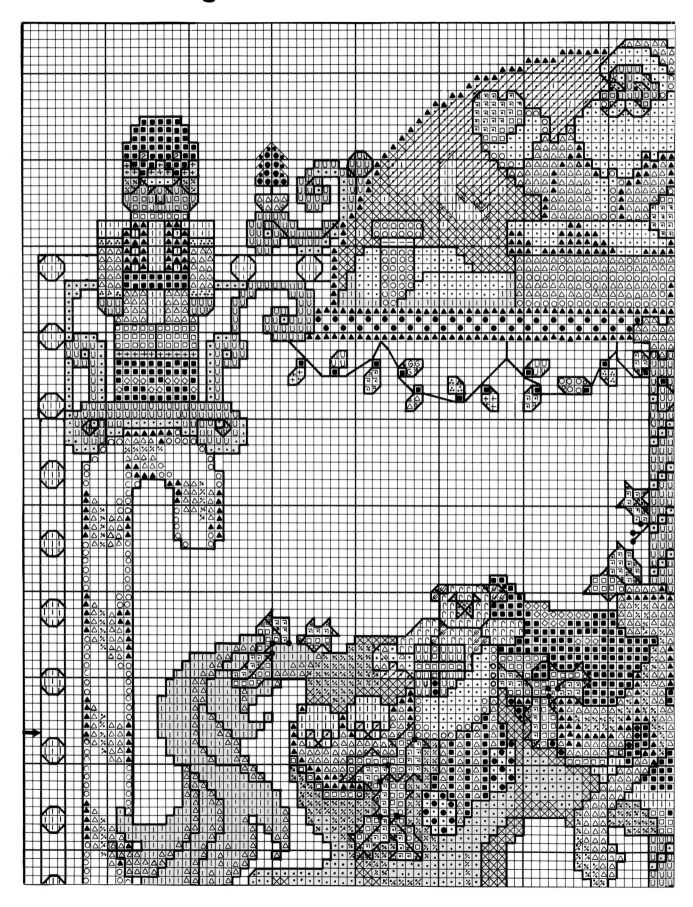

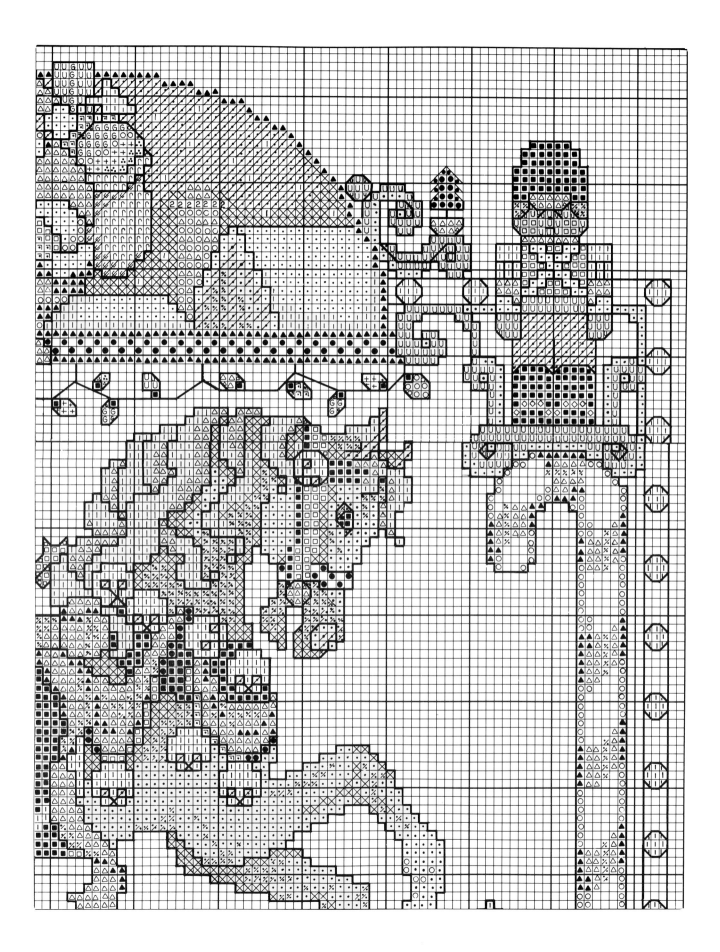

December Delights

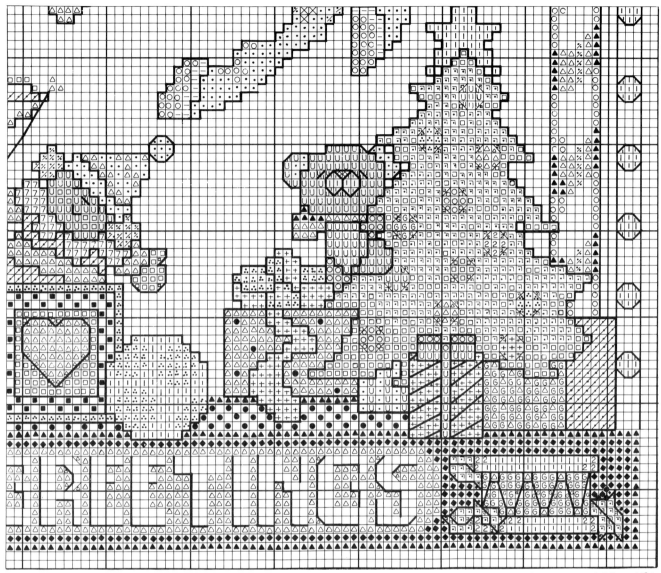

Stitch Count: 152 x 161

December Delights

Model (see photo)
Stitched on white Aida 14, the finished design size is 10⅞" x 11½". The fabric was cut 17" x 18".

FABRICS	DESIGN SIZES
Aida 11	13⅞" x 14⅝"
Aida 18	8½" x 9"
Hardanger 22	6⅞" x 7⅜"

Anchor			DMC (used for sample)

Step 1: Cross-stitch (2 strands)

Anchor			DMC	
1				White
301			744	Yellow-pale
306			725	Topaz
307			783	Christmas Gold
881			945	Peach Beige
347			402	Mahogany-vy. lt.
324			922	Copper-lt.
349			921	Copper
316			740	Tangerine
333			608	Orange Red
46			666	Christmas Red-bright
22			816	Garnet
24			776	Pink-med.
85			3609	Plum-ultra lt.
86			3608	Plum-vy. lt.
87			3607	Plum-lt.
110			208	Lavender-vy. dk.
433			996	Electric Blue-med.
131			798	Delft-dk.
133			796	Royal Blue-dk.
185			964	Seagreen-lt.
256			704	Chartreuse-bright
239			702	Kelly Green
923			699	Christmas Green
246			895	Christmas Green-dk.
885			739	Tan-ultra vy. lt.
362			437	Tan-lt.
376			842	Beige Brown-vy. lt.
378			841	Beige Brown-lt.
352			300	Mahogany-vy. dk.
398			415	Pearl Gray
400			414	Steel Gray-dk.
401			413	Pewter Gray-dk.
403			310	Black

Step 2: Backstitch (1 strand)

Anchor		DMC	
46		666	Christmas Red-bright (tree pots, hair bows on doll, nose, hearts)
22		816	Garnet (ribbon on horse)
110		208	Lavender-vy. dk. (bow on yellow package)
923		699	Christmas Green (leaves, stems, trees, Santa's gloves)
352		300	Mahogany-vy. dk. (scrollwork, soldiers' arms, yellow balls, star, horse, jingle bells, French horn, pole, rooftops, Santa's sack, gift and drum outlines)
401		413	Pewter Gray-dk. (all white on Santa, chimneys, soldiers, horse hooves, candy canes, bears, stocking cuff on horse, giraffe, baby doll, jack-in-the-box, streamers, presents, ball)
403		310	Black (all else)

Step 3: Long Stitch (1 strand)

Anchor		DMC	
306		725	Topaz (red drum)
46		666	Christmas Red-bright (yellow package stripes, blue drum)
923		699	Christmas Green (pine needles)
352		300	Mahogany-vy. dk. (on jingle bells)
401		413	Pewter Gray-dk. (streamer stick)
403		310	Black (lights)

Step 4: French Knot (1 strand)

Anchor		DMC	
46		666	Christmas Red-bright

Attention!

Model (see photo)
The two soldier motifs are from the top left and right corners of "December Delights" on pages 116–120. Stitched on white Jobelan 28 over 2 threads, the finished design size is 2⅜" x 2⅜" for one soldier. Center horizontally and begin stitching 2" below top edge. Stitch to fill cuff as desired. The fabric was cut 24" x 11". The stitch count is 14 x 33 for each soldier.

FABRICS	DESIGN SIZES
Aida 11	1¼" x 3"
Aida 14	1" x 2⅜".
Aida 18	¾" x 1⅞"
Hardanger 22	⅝" x 1½"

Materials

Completed design on white Jobelan 28; matching thread
6½"-high papier-mâché boot
Two 17¾" x 4½" batting pieces
Red and black acrylic paint
Pearl lustre spray paint
½ yard of 1"-wide cotton trim

Paint brush
Sandpaper
Glue

Directions
Seams are ¼".

1. Sand seams of papier-mâché boot lightly. Paint boot top red and sole black; allow to dry. Spray boot with pearl lustre. Repeat to achieve desired effect.

2. Cut design piece to 17¾" x 8½" with design 2" below top edge and centered horizontally.

3. For cuff, stitch 8½" ends of design piece with right sides facing. Fold in half with long raw edges aligned and design right side out. Insert one batting layer inside folded cuff. (Use second layer, if needed, to keep cuff smooth over boot edges.) Stitch.

4. Slide cuff over boot top, placing design as desired. Fold cuff 1" to inside of boot; glue. Glue trim over raw edges on inside of boot.

Christmas Cheer

Model (see photo)
The tree motif is from "December Delights" on pages 116–120. Stitched on daffodil Pastel Linen 28 over 2 threads, the finished design size is 3½" x 3⅝". The fabric was cut 10" x 10". The tree stitch count is 49 x 51.

FABRICS	DESIGN SIZES
Aida 11	4½" x 4⅝"
Aida 14	3½" x 3⅝"
Aida 18	2¾" x 2⅞"
Hardanger 22	2¼" x 2⅜"

Materials

Completed design on daffodil Pastel Linen 28; matching thread
¼ yard red pindot fabric
4¾" fleece square

Directions
Seams are ¼".

1. Cut design piece to 4¾" square. From pindot fabric, cut 1¼"-wide bias strips, piecing as needed to make ¾ yard of binding.

2. Layer coaster back (wrong side up), fleece and coaster front (right side up) with raw edges aligned; stitch. Trim seam allowance.

3. With right sides facing and raw edges aligned, stitch binding to front, over stitching line. Stitch to, but not through, seam allowance; backstitch. Fold bias at a 90° angle to stitched edge and turn corner. Resume stitching, meeting the backstitch at seam allowance. Fold bias to back, turning under seam allowance. Slipstitch, covering stitch line of binding and mitering each corner on both sides of fabric. See diagrams on page 113.

Handfuls Of Fun

Models (see photo)
Each mitten motif is from "December Delights" on pages 116–120.

Jack-in-the-box: Stitched on Wedgwood Murano 30 over 2 threads, the finished design size is 1⅝" x 2¼". The fabric was cut 9" x 11". The jack-in-the-box stitch count is 24 x 33.

FABRICS	DESIGN SIZES
Aida 11	2⅛" x 3"
Aida 14	1¾" x 2⅜"
Aida 18	1⅜" x 1⅞"
Hardanger 22	1⅛" x 1½"

Giraffe: Stitched on moss green Murano 30 over 2 threads, the finished design size is 1¼" x 1⅞". The fabric was cut 9" x 11". The giraffe stitch count is 18 x 28.

FABRICS	DESIGN SIZES
Aida 11	1⅝" x 2½"
Aida 14	1¼" x 2"
Aida 18	1" x 1½"
Hardanger 22	⅞" x 1¼"

Girl: Stitched on white Murano 30 over 2 threads, the finished design size is 1⅜" x 1¼". The fabric was cut 9" x 11". The girl stitch count is 20 x 18.

FABRICS	DESIGN SIZES
Aida 11	1⅞" x 1⅝"
Aida 14	1⅜" x 1¼"
Aida 18	1⅛" x 1"
Hardanger 22	⅞" x ⅞"

Materials (for one mitten pair)
Two completed designs on Murano 30;
  matching thread
Two 5" x 6" matching unstitched
  Murano 30 pieces
10" of ⅛"-wide blue satin ribbon;
  matching thread
Tracing paper
Dressmaker's pen
Polyester stuffing

Directions (for one mitten pair)
Seams are ¼".

1. Make pattern. With designs centered on each design piece, cut two opposite mittens according to pattern. Zigzag edges to control raveling. Cut two opposite mittens from unstitched Murano. Zigzag edges.

2. With right sides facing and thumbs matching, stitch together one stitched and one unstitched mitten, leaving the straight edge open. Carefully clip seam allowances around thumb. Turn right side out. Stuff mitten and slipstitch opening closed. Sew a running stitch parallel to and ½" from straight edge. Gather slightly, securing thread. Repeat for remaining mitten.

3. Tack ribbon to side seam opposite thumb on each mitten.

Mitten Pattern

Metric Conversion Chart

MM - Millimeters   CM - Centimeters

INCHES TO MILLIMETERS AND CENTIMETERS

INCHES	MM	CM	INCHES	CM	INCHES	CM
⅛	3	0.3	9	22.9	30	76.2
¼	6	0.6	10	25.4	31	78.7
⅜	10	1.0	11	27.9	32	81.3
½	13	1.3	12	30.5	33	83.8
⅝	16	1.6	13	33.0	34	86.4
¾	19	1.9	14	35.6	35	88.9
⅞	22	2.2	15	38.1	36	91.4
1	25	2.5	16	40.6	37	94.0
1¼	32	3.2	17	43.2	38	96.5
1½	38	3.8	18	45.7	39	99.1
1¾	44	4.4	19	48.3	40	101.6
2	51	5.1	20	50.8	41	104.1
2½	64	6.4	21	53.3	42	106.7
3	76	7.6	22	55.9	43	109.2
3½	89	8.9	23	58.4	44	111.8
4	102	10.2	24	61.0	45	114.3
4½	114	11.4	25	63.5	46	116.8
5	127	12.7	26	66.0	47	119.4
6	152	15.2	27	68.6	48	121.9
7	178	17.8	28	71.1	49	124.5
8	203	20.3	29	73.7	50	127.0

YARDS TO METERS

Yards	Meters	Yards	Meters	Yards	Meters	Yards	Meters	Yards	Meters
⅛	0.11	2⅛	1.94	4⅛	3.77	6⅛	5.60	8⅛	7.43
¼	0.23	2¼	2.06	4¼	3.89	6¼	5.72	8¼	7.54
⅜	0.34	2⅜	2.17	4⅜	4.00	6⅜	5.83	8⅜	7.66
½	0.46	2½	2.29	4½	4.11	6½	5.94	8½	7.77
⅝	0.57	2⅝	2.40	4⅝	4.23	6⅝	6.06	8⅝	7.89
¾	0.69	2¾	2.51	4¾	4.34	6¾	6.17	8¾	8.00
⅞	0.80	2⅞	2.63	4⅞	4.46	6⅞	6.29	8⅞	8.12
1	0.91	3	2.74	5	4.57	7	6.40	9	8.23
1⅛	1.03	3⅛	2.86	5⅛	4.69	7⅛	6.52	9⅛	8.34
1¼	1.14	3¼	2.97	5¼	4.80	7¼	6.63	9¼	8.46
1⅜	1.26	3⅜	3.09	5⅜	4.91	7⅜	6.74	9⅜	8.57
1½	1.37	3½	3.20	5½	5.03	7½	6.86	9½	8.69
1⅝	1.49	3⅝	3.31	5⅝	5.14	7⅝	6.97	9⅝	8.80
1¾	1.60	3¾	3.43	5¾	5.26	7¾	7.09	9¾	8.92
1⅞	1.71	3⅞	3.54	5⅞	5.37	7⅞	7.20	9⅞	9.03
2	1.83	4	3.66	6	5.49	8	7.32	10	9.14

126

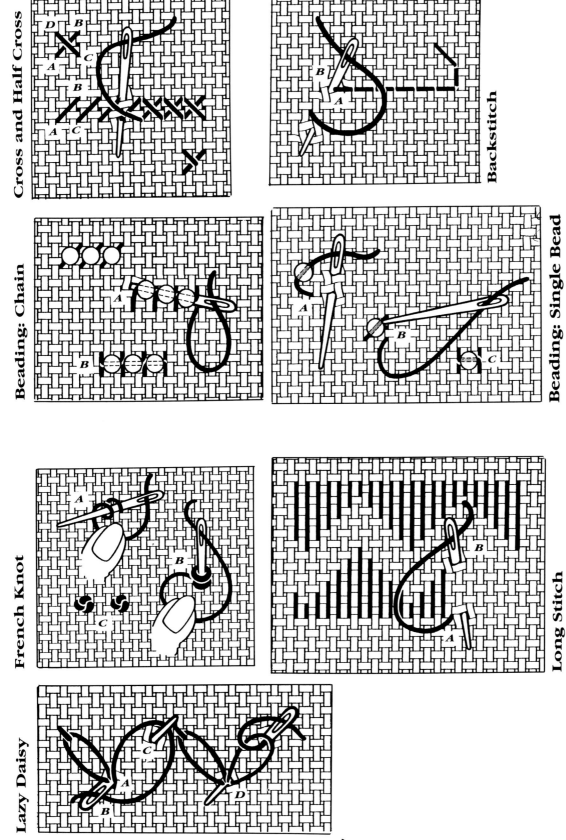

Cross and Half Cross

Backstitch

Beading: Chain

Beading: Single Bead

French Knot

Long Stitch

Lazy Daisy

Special Stitches

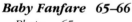